Cybersecurity:

The Hacker Proof Guide To Cybersecurity, Internet Safety, Cybercrime, & Preventing Attacks

Claim Your Free Bonus

Master the Art of Memory Improvement with Brain Training to Learn Faster, Remember More, Increase Productivity and Improve Memory

If you've ever found yourself forgetting things then you have probably wished that your memory was better.

It transpires that there is no so such thing as a "bad" memory. There are merely people who don't use their memories to the fullest potential.

Improve your memory...read this book!

Table of Contents

Cyber Defense Plus Cyber Resilience

Conclusion

Introduction

US $600 billion a year. That's the estimated cost of cybercrime as of 2018. That's a $100 billion increase since 2014, which was the last time a similar study was released by the Center for Strategic and International Studies and McAfee. This new estimate is around 0.8% of the global GDP, compared to 0.7 from 2014.

Cybercrime is never tiring, it hasn't diminished, and there are no signs of it stopping in the near future. Why? Because cybercriminals find it easy and very much rewarding. Plus, the chances of getting caught and being punished seem low.

Now that we know cybercrime isn't going away anytime soon, the only thing we can do is to get ourselves protected.

This is where cybersecurity steps in.

This book is aimed at people who want to gain knowledge of the essentials of cybersecurity and how it can be used to protect against cybercrimes. The knowledge from this book can be used to protect companies and individuals against cyberattacks.

Chapter 1. Cybersecurity – A Brief History

Most people assume that the term cybersecurity has just been coined in the last decade and it's something new. However, its history goes back to the '70s. It's a time when most people didn't have a computer. There are even 'hacking' incidents' that have happened before the existence of computers. But for the purpose of this book, let's talk about what happened in an experiment in 1971.

The Very First Computer Worm

Bob Thomas created a program in 1971 that is now considered the very first computer worm. This worm was programmed to bounce between computers, which at that time was groundbreaking. It was not even malicious, unlike the computer worms of today. What it does is display a message on the screen of the infected computer that says 'I'm the creeper: catch me if you can.'

The dawn of this vulnerability in computers gave birth to more complex attacks that were meant to be malicious and some were downright destructive.

The Very First Denial-of-Service Attack

Robert Morris created a special computer worm in 1989 which slowed down the Internet significantly back in those days, making connections unavailable. This was the first denial-of-service or DoS recorded in history. Morris didn't even develop the worm to wreak havoc. The original motive behind the worm is to expose security flaws like weak passwords and Unix Sendmail. However, the worm replicated excessively which caused the Internet connection slowdown and damages amounting to somewhere between $100,000 and $10,000,000. The Internet even became partitioned for several days because of the anomaly.

The AIDS Trojan

The same year the first DoS attack was made also marked the introduction of the first ransomware attack initiated by Joseph Popp. He developed a malware which he nicknames the AIDS Trojan. This malware was distributed via Joseph's mailing lists and by using floppy disks. With the Trojan malware, he was expecting to extort money out of people who want to regain access to their files, which were lost due to how ransomware is programmed. Extortion is the goal of modern ransomware attack, hence the name. The AIDS Trojan wasn't really successful because it was poorly designed and can be removed easily. It only scrambled filenames instead of the contents so infected computers were still usable and programs such as AIDS_OUT were developed to unlock the files.

The Computer Misuse Act

With the proliferation of attacks on computers, the United Kingdom created one of the first acts or legislation in history meant to deal with cybersecurity. It was titled The Computer Misuse Act which was passed in 1990. According to the act, any unauthorized attempt to access any computer system is illegal. The Computer Misuse Act is still active though a lot of amendments have been added to modernize it.

Security Becomes Mainstream

1999 saw the birth of Microsoft's new operating system, Windows 98. It was highly successful and made computers easier to use for common people. This spike in the ownership and use of computers also made software security systems more common. Microsoft released a lot of patches and commercial security products developed for Windows. Third-party security vendors also joined the bandwagon and released their own anti-hacking software to be used for home computers.

ILOVEYOU Virus

Microsoft also dominated the office applications market during the late 90s and early 2000s with its bundle called Microsoft Office. Included with Microsoft Office is the email application called Microsoft Outlook. And this application is what a virus released in 2000 exploited. The virus is attached to an email with the note saying 'I LOVE YOU'. Once the attachment is opened it replicates the same email and attachment and sends it to all the email addresses of the recipient's contacts list in Microsoft Outlook, propagating exponentially. This attack was so effective that it infected 45 million users in one day making it one of the most damaging viruses in the history of cybersecurity.

The Creation of Homeland Security

The Department of Homeland Security was created by a bill filed by George W. Bush in 2002. This governing body took on the country's IT infrastructure responsibilities. Later on, a division of the department was created specifically for cybersecurity.

Hacktivism

Although hacking was mainly born out of extorting money or stealing data, some hackers used their knowledge and tools to bring about change and influence policies. Their goal was to increase political awareness through Internet activism which is their way of spreading their ideals. Thus, hacktivism was born. One of the more famous hacktivists groups is called Anonymous and they have initiated cyberattacks against organizations and governments.

Wikileaks

The Wikileaks of 2016 is by far the most infamous leak of information in history done via the Internet. Documents coming from the 2016 national committee were published for the whole world to see. The whole scandal involved hackers from the Russian intelligence agency.

The Future

The application of cybersecurity is here to stay. In 2018, we witnessed some of the most culturally notable and largest cyberattacks in recent history and we have learned a lot. We now know that Facebook is selling our personal data. The Marriott Hotel fiasco showed that breaches in security can remain dormant and unnoticed for years.

There is more to come and we, as upholders of cybersecurity, should always be ready. Passwords are dying a slow death with the introduction of Multi-Factor Authentication systems and the rise in the use of Artificial Intelligence makes detecting and preventing cybercrimes more efficient.

Chapter 2. Common Cybersecurity Attacks

No two battles in history are exactly alike. Yet, similar tactics and strategies have been used mainly because they are effective as time has proven.

The same way of thinking applies to hacking. When hackers are trying to infiltrate an organization, they'll use the same time-proven tools and distribution channels. They will use the same hacking techniques that are proven to be highly effective like phishing, malware, or cross-site-scripting.

Here are some of the most common cybersecurity attacks seen today.

Phishing

Most people now know better than to open an attachment from a random email or click any link embedded in it. There has to be a valid reason for you to take that course of action.

Unfortunately, attackers also know this. So in order to make you give out sensitive information or install malware on your system, they employ phishing strategies. Phishing is basically the sender pretending to be something or someone else to entice you to take that action that you wouldn't, in more suspicious scenarios. Phishing relies on natural human impulses and curiosity which makes this kind of attack hard to stop.

During phishing, the attacker may send an email your way but will make it appear as though it's coming from a person or entity you trust, such as your boss or an organization you're doing business with. This email will, in all sense, seem legitimate and may stir some sense of urgency in you. An example would be a suspicious activity coming from your account.

Phishing emails usually contain an attachment that can be opened or a link that can be clicked. Opening the attachment installs the malware in your system and clicking the link takes you a website that may look legitimate, asking for your account and password to open an important file. But this website is actually a trap that is designed to capture your credentials after you log in.

Combatting phishing attacks requires recognizing the importance of verifying links or attachments as well as the email senders.

Malware

You clicked a malicious attachment mistakenly and you see the antivirus alert screen pop up. You just had a close encounter with malware and luckily, your security software protected you.

The term 'malware' represents various forms of malicious or harmful software like viruses and ransomware. Attackers use malware to get access to computers and eventually all the computers in the office network and it can be effective.

Once the malware gets inside your computer it can do anything from getting control of the machine, to recording all your keystrokes and actions, to sending confidential data from the computer or the whole network silently to the attacker's system.

There are a variety of methods that attackers can use to install malware on your computer but it often requires you to take action. That's why it's usually associated with phishing which lures you into opening an attachment or clicking a link to a malicious website.

SQL Injection Attack

SQL, or structured query language, is a programming language mainly used to work with databases. Most servers that host critical data for services like websites use this language to manage the information stored in the databases.

SQL injection attacks are specifically targeted to SQL servers and attackers do it through the use of malicious code to instruct the server to give out information that it shouldn't in a normal scenario.

This becomes critical if the database server is hosting private customer information like usernames, passwords, credit card numbers, or other identifiable information, which can be lucrative and tempting targets for attackers.

The SQL injection attack is done by exploiting known vulnerabilities in SQL allowing the database server to execute malicious code. If an SQL server has been found by an attacker to be vulnerable to an SQL injection attack, the attacker can just type in code in the website's search box which would force the database server to transfer the stored usernames and password for that particular site.

Cross-Site Scripting or XSS

SQL injection attacks go for stored data on the server or website itself like sensitive financial information or user credentials. The Cross-Site Scripting attack, on the other hand, directly target the users of a website.

This attack is similar to an SQL injection attack in the manner that malicious code is also injected into the website but is also different because it does not attack the website itself. What happens is that the injected malicious code will only run in the browser of the user when the compromised website is visited, going after the user directly and not the website.

For example, the attacker deploys an XSS attack by embedding malicious code into the comment box using a script that is automatically executed when the user replies to the comment.

Cross-site scripting attacks damage a website's reputation because it can expose users' information and there is no indication that malicious activity has even occurred. Sensitive information sent by the visitor to the site like credit card data, credentials, or other personal information can be hijacked using this attack. The website owners might not even realize the problem exists.

Man-in-the-Middle and Session Hijacking Attacks

When you access information across the Internet, your computer takes care of tiny background transactions that go back-and-forth between servers and this is what lets the system know who you are and that you're requesting specific services or websites.

Once this validation has been established, the servers respond by providing the information you requested. This whole process happens in every transaction you engage with on the Internet such as browsing or logging into a site using your credentials.

A unique session ID is provided between your computer and the server from which you are accessing the information and this information stays private between the two systems.

However, this session can be hijacked by an attacker by capturing the private session ID and pretending to be the computer making the request. This allows the attacker to log in as you and gain access to information that only you should have. The attacker can user cross-site scripting attack methods to capture the session ID.

In another method, attackers can also hijack the session and put themselves in the middle of the user and the server pretending to be both parties. This allows attackers to capture information coming and going to and from both directions. This is referred to as a man-in-the-middle attack.

Denial-of-Service

Imagine driving on a single lane country road which normally doesn't see more than one car at any given time. But somehow, there's a major sporting event and a country fair going on at the same time and this is the only road that can be used by the visitors. The road isn't designed to handle such heavy traffic so vehicles get stalled and no one is able to leave.

That is what happens when a denial-of-service or DoS attack is targeting a website. An attacker floods the website with traffic that it wasn't designed to handle, overloading the webserver and making it almost impossible for the server to provide content to the visitors.

This can also happen in a non-malicious scenario such as massive news story breaking and a lot of people visit a newspaper's website overloading the server with requests for more information. However, this kind is often malicious in nature wherein an attacker shuts down a server for legitimate users by injecting overwhelming network traffic.

DoS attacks can be performed by more than one computer simultaneously, which is called Distributed Denial-of-Service Attack or DDoS. When this happens, defending from the attack and identifying the attacker can be more difficult because they are coming from different sources from all over the world.

Credential Reuse

With so many websites to visit which require credentials to access the service you require, it can be tempting to use the same credentials to some of the sites to make your life easier. Security best practices highly recommend that you don't do this, though and require you to use at least unique passwords for all the websites you visit and applications you use. Still, many people reuse their credentials and this is something attackers really like.

When attackers have collected users' credentials from a compromised website or database server, or sometimes through black market websites, they know that using the same usernames and passwords on other websites has a high chance of working.

Remember that your bank's website, your favorite tech forum, or social media can be hacked and if you're using the same credentials on all those sites, the attackers now have access to financial and personal information.

Variety is important when we're talking about credentials. Use password management applications to help you managed the credentials you use.

So what do you do against these attacks?

In the next chapters, we'll discuss the different forms of these attacks so you can recognize each one and learn how to keep yourself from being a victim.

Chapter 3. Phishing Attack

Phishing is a type of cybersecurity attack wherein attackers attempt to entice targets to divulge valuable or sensitive information. In this attack, the users' credentials, company data, financial information and any data that can be of value are the targets. Some phishing attacks can be easy to identify but some forms can be hard to spot.

Types of Phishing

Phishing attacks are usually aimed at many users or potential targets. A 'quantity over quality' approach is employed and it requires minimal effort and preparation from the attackers. They're also expecting that at least a small portion of the users will fall into the trap. Likewise, the expected gain is usually not that big.

Phishing attacks usually lure the users by tapping into their desires in order to solicit an action (usually done through a mouse click). Examples are:

- You could win a free gift card to Store X (greed)

- Your request for loan has been approved (confusion)

- To avoid account cancellation, please login immediately (sense of urgency or concern)

Phishing attacks have evolved through the years and attackers have become more innovative these days. Variations of the phishing attack may require more effort from the attackers but the payout is higher per victim or more victims fall into the trap. Here are some of the types of phishing attacks.

Spear Phishing

When an attacker customizes a phishing attack for a specific individual or organization, it's called spear phishing. The attack will require additional information that is gathered by the attacker ahead of time and the incorporation of familiar elements like website and email addresses of the company or its partners, company logos, and even personal or professional details of the target. All of these make the email seem authentic and the additional effort leads to a higher payoff or more victims being duped.

Whaling

This is another variation of the phishing attack but instead of going for the rank-and-file personnel, whaling targets the senior executives of the organization. Attacks take into consideration the specific roles and responsibilities of these people and send focused messages to trick them. If a whaling attack becomes successful, the effect on the targeted company can be devastating because the attackers may gain access to the company accounts and secrets.

Clone Phishing

In clone phishing, targets are sent a clone or a copy of a legitimate email that they received earlier, but some changes have been made with the original content in order to lure the target. Examples of changes are invalid URL links or malicious attachments. Because the targets have seen the email before and the previous one was legit, they are more likely to believe the cloned email.

More Phishing Variations

As users learn how to detect and thwart phishing attacks, attackers also continue to work on creative ways to fool the unsuspecting computer users. In one recent incident, attackers sent a Google Doc to a user by spoofing the email address of another user known to the victim. Opening the link gives access to the Google login credentials of the target and also sends the same email to all the email addresses in the victim's address book thus, propagating the attack.

Phishing Techniques

There are a number of mechanisms that attackers can use to phish targets such as social media, email, texting, instant messaging, and compromised websites. There are even attacks involving phone calls. No matter what the delivery mechanism is, there are certain techniques used by attackers.

Link Spoofing

One common technique attackers use in phishing is called link spoofing. In this technique, the attackers make a malicious URL look like the legitimate one. This is in the hope that users will not notice the difference and click it. Some manipulated links are easy to identify especially to those users who check thoroughly before clicking e.g. bankingusa.com vs bank1ngusa.com. Some attackers, though, use homograph attacks wherein characters that look alike are used, reducing the effectiveness of visual detection.

Website Spoofing

Websites can also be forged or spoofed to appear like authentic ones. This is done by using Javascript or Flash which allows attackers to manipulate how the URL is shown to the user. So for the eyes of the visitor, the website will seem legit with all the characters appearing properly but the website is actually malicious. Using Cross-Site Scripting, vulnerabilities in the website itself can be exploited so the authentic website is presented while the credentials of the users are stolen without being detected.

Redirects

Using redirects, attackers can have the user's browser to communicate with another website. In a malicious redirect, visitors willingly visit a website but are then forcibly redirected to a website controlled by the attacker. This is done by compromising a legitimate website using redirection code or through a discovered vulnerability in the website that will then allow forced redirection using specially crafted URLs.

Covert redirects are less obvious than malicious redirects because the users still see the authentic website. The website has actually been compromised and some action buttons may have been changed to capture user credentials and send them to the attacker's email before redirecting to the actual website.

Preventing Phishing Attacks

Here are some tips to prevent phishing attacks from happening.

Continuous Education and Training

User education is still the best way to fight off phishing and this should be done to all users from the top ranks down to the bottom. Security awareness training should be done periodically and the content updated with the latest innovations in phishing attacks. The security team may also implement 'phishing exercises' to increase knowledge and help users learn how to identify phishing attacks as they happen.

Filtering Attachments

Use an attachment filtering application to detect and quarantine attachments that are commonly utilized in phishing attacks. This can also be done using your corporate email policies. By doing this, malicious attachments don't reach the users' mailboxes.

Filtering URLs

There are applications that can be used to quarantine messages with malicious URLs embedded. These applications also resolve URLs from link shorteners like bit.ly, goo.gl, and others.

To bypass these filters, attackers may send phishing emails that don't contain text but a large picture that contains the text. This attack can be prevented by using filters with character recognition technology.

Enforce Proper Credential Management

You may disallow weak passwords in your network. This can be done through authentication policies wherein passwords will require minimum lengths, special characters, the user of numbers and small and capital letters, periodic password change, disabling password reuse, and others.

Using multi-factor authentication or MFA can also be implemented in your network so that an additional layer security, which the company has control of, is used which makes hacking the password useless.

Regular virus and malware scans

Antivirus and anti-malware applications should be kept updated with the latest signatures. Regular and periodic deep scan should also be done on all systems in the network.

Patches and updates

When a vulnerability is discovered, developers of operating systems and applications release updates to patch it. That's why it's important to keep abreast of the latest updates and patches for your systems.

There are many ways attackers can and will try to lure users into their trap via phishing and it may all sound scary. But with regular training and education on what phishing attacks exist and how they can be prevented, you minimize the possibility of an attack doing significant damage to the company's systems.

Chapter 4. SQL Injection Attacks

SQL injection, or SQLi attacks target database servers using SQL statements specially crafted to trick the system into behaving undesirably and unexpectedly. Once compromised, the attacker can do such things as stealing data, bypassing authentication, deleting data, corrupting or modifying data, gaining root access, and running arbitrary code on the system.

SQL Injection Attack Types

There are a number of ways that a SQL injection attack can be carried out by an attacker. Before choosing an attack method or vector, the attacker first observes the system's behavior.

Unsanitized Input

This is a pretty common SQLi attack utilized by attackers wherein a user input is provided that isn't sanitized for particular characters or not validated as expected or correct.

Blind SQL Injection

Also known as the Inferential SQLi, the Blind SQLi attack doesn't show the information directly from the database being queried. HTTP responses and how long the database takes to respond are carefully analyzed by the attacker which then provides clues on how to compromise the database.

Out-of-Band Injection

This attack is complex and is usually employed by attackers as last resort when all the other single, direct attacks didn't work. To do this, the attacker crafts specific SQL statements that are sent to the database. This triggers the system to establish a connection to another database server being controlled by the attacker. Using this method, the attacker can then extract data from the database or even control its behavior.

Another type of Out-of-Band Injection attack is called the Second Order Injection. An SQL injection statement is stored and then executed by a separate action of the database server. This action could be a scheduled job or maintenance and executed by a database admin account. When this action is initiated, that's the time the database system connects to the attacker-controlled server.

Preventing SQL Injection Attacks

Here are some suggestions on how to prevent SQL injection attacks from being successful:

Avoid using Dynamic SQL

- Don't use user-provided input into SQL statements directly.

- Prefer safer SQL inputs such as parameterized queries and prepared statements.

- Instead of dynamic SQL, use stored procedures instead which are considered safer and more difficult to exploit.

Clean user-provided inputs

- Ensure that characters that are supposed to be escaped are indeed escaped properly.

- Confirm that the type expected exactly matches that of the data type submitted.

Sensitive data should not be left in plaintext

- Stored confidential or private information in the database should be encrypted.

- Encrypting data provides another layer of security in case an attacker is able to get hold of it.

Database privileges and permissions should be limited

- Ensure that only the minimum required capabilities or access is assigned to the database users.

- This ensures that even though an attacker gains access to the system, the action or damage that can be done is limited.

Don't display database errors to the users directly

- Error messages can serve as clues to attackers on the type and status of your databases and use this information to stage an appropriate attack.

If web applications need to access databases, utilize a Web Application Firewall or WAF

- A WAF can provide protection to applications that are web-facing

- It can be used to identify if there are ongoing SQL injection attacks

- Depending on how the WAF is set up, it can even prevent SQLi attacks from reaching the database or the application.

Routinely check your web applications using a web application security testing solution especially if they interact with databases

- New regressions or bugs can be discovered over time and doing periodic testing can help you catch and patch them accordingly.

Patch database servers and databases using the latest available updates

- Attackers are always finding ways to infiltrate and they do this by looking for known weaknesses or vulnerabilities in your database system. Developers release updates and patches as these holes are found so ensure that they are installed as soon as possible.

SQL injection attacks are common and even pretty popular. Ensure that you are taking essential measures in keeping the data secure by installing the latest updates or patches, testing and protecting your web applications, and encrypting your data.

Chapter 5. Cross-Site Scripting

Cross-site scripting or XSS is a type of code injection attack wherein attackers embed malicious client-side scripts in the user's web browser where it can be executed. These attacks are not targeted directly and rely on vulnerabilities found on web applications and websites to execute the malicious script when a user unknowingly interact with the compromised website.

When a compromised website is visited by an unsuspecting user, the script is loaded by the browser and executed. The script can be designed to steal or extract sensitive or personal data, hijack sessions, and more. JavaScript is one of the most widely used web scripting languages and it has become a favorite amongst attackers. But XSS attacks can be designed for any web scripting language available as long as it is supported by a browser. XSS attacks have been around for more than a decade and have remained to be popular amongst hackers because they are highly effective and fairly easy to implement.

Type of XSS Attacks
Reflected XSS

This type of XSS attack requires a vulnerable website that accepts data using a malicious script that is sent by the user's web browser which then 'attacks' the target. It's also referred to as a non-persistent attack since the malicious script is not saved in on the vulnerable site but sent by the browser itself.

One example of a reflected XSS attack might involve a URL crafted by an attacker that passes a tiny maligned script a one query parameter sent to a site that has an XSS-vulnerable search page.

http://vulnerable-site.com/search?search_term="<script>(i am a malicious script)</script>"

The attacker just then needs to have users visiting this URL using their browsers. This can be done through phishing with an email that contains the maligned URL or just publish the URL to a non-vulnerable, public website for users to click.

When the link is clicked by the target, the vulnerable website receives the embedded query parameter. The target is expecting that the value is something he or she is interested in but in fact, it's the malicious script. The search page will display normally as any other search page would but because the site is vulnerable, the malicious script is accepted by the browser and executes it.

Persistent XSS

Opposite to reflected XSS, the persistent XSS attack requires that the malicious code be stored (thus persisting) on the vulnerable site itself. Visitors of that site are then attacked when they interact with the site.

An example of the persistent XSS attack is a message posted in a forum by an attacker on a vulnerable site. The post will contain the malicious script which, if visited by a user will be loaded by the browser and executed.

The main difference between persistent and reflected XSS attack is that the former see all users of the vulnerable website as targets.

DOM-Based XSS

This another kind of XSS attack which exploits the vulnerability in client-side scripts being to visitors by the site or application. The difference of a DOM-based XSS attack compared to a persistent of reflected XSS attack is that the vulnerable site does not server the malicious script to the user's browser directly. Instead, it's the site's vulnerable client-side script that does the job. That means the malicious script is not stored on the vulnerable, similar to a reflected XSS attack.

A DOM-bases XSS attack happens in a scenario similar to a reflected XSS attack. A malicious script is embedded in a URL created by an attacker which is then distributed to potential targets. When the URL is clicked, the browser loads both the search page and the vulnerable client-side script. The site does not produce the page with the malicious script. It's the client-side processing script that causes the user's browser to load and then execute the malicious script. This attack shows that XSS exploits are not limited to sites but can also affect browsers.

Preventing XSS Attacks

To help protect the users from XSS attacks, follow these suggestions:

Sanitize the user input

- Use validation in order to detect user-provided input that can be potentially malicious

- Prevent potentially malicious data provided by the users from being automatically executed by the browser by encoding the output

Limit the use of user-provided data

- Ensure that it's only used when really necessary

Use Content Security Policy

- It's an added security layer designed to detect some attacks including XSS and mitigate them

XSS attacks are a popular vector because of the high success rate but you can keep your web site from being vulnerable through thoughtful testing and design.

Chapter 6. Man-in-the-Middle Attacks

Man-in-the-middle attacks allow perpetrators to 'listen' in on the transfer of data between two targets and these attacks are very common. The attack is initiated between two systems that are communicating legitimately which captures the data send to and from both targets, thus earning the moniker 'main-in-the-middle.'

Here's an analogy of what happens during a man-in-the-middle attack:

Sandra and Chris are conversing over Facebook Messenger. Mark wants to eavesdrop but he doesn't want either of the parties to know. Mark will tell Sandra that he's Chris and also tell Chris that he's Sandra. That way, Sandra thinks that she's speaking to Chris and gives out information that only Chris should know. Mark can then pass the information to Chris (who's thinking he's conversing with Sandra). Mark is then able to hijack the conversation between Sandra and Chris transparently.

Types of Man-in-the-Middle (MITM) Attacks
ARP Spoofing

Address Resolution Protocol or ARP is used in resolving IP addresses to corresponding physical or media access control (MAC) addresses in a network. When a particular host needs to communicate with a given IP address, the ARP cache is referenced in order to translate that IP address into a matching MAC address. If the address is not yet in the ARP cache, a request will be made which will ask for the MAC address of that device owning the IP address.

An attacker who wants to pose as a different host can reply to requests that it should not be replying to using its MAC address.

Using data packets that are precisely placed, the attacker can capture the data flowing between the two hosts. Important information can be gathered from the captured data which may include the session token exchange which will then give full access to some application accounts the attackers should not have access to.

DNS Spoofing

While ARP translates IP addresses to MAC addresses, DNS translates domain names into IP addresses. In a DNS spoofing attack, the perpetrator uses corrupted DNS cache information on a host to try and access a different host using that host's domain name, e.g. www.onlinebank.com. The user visiting this site will think this is a trusted source and sends sensitive information. When the IP address has already been spoofed by an attacker, DNS spoofing becomes easier.

Rogue Access Point

Wireless devices will usually try to connect to an access point with the strongest signal. An attacker can set up a rogue wireless access point which will trick wireless devices within the range to join the domain. The attacker can then manipulate the network traffic of the victim. The attacker doesn't have to connect to a trusted network to implement this attack. They simply need to be within the range of the wireless network they want to spoof.

mDNS Spoofing

Multicast DNS or mDNS uses broadcast methodology the same way ARP does that's why it's an excellent target for a spoofing attack. mDNS is supposed to simplify network device configuration in a Local Area Network or LAN. Users need not know the addresses of the device they need to communicate with because the system will do the resolution. This protocol is mostly used in entertainment systems, printers, and TVs because these are usually inside a trusted network. When an application tries to find a device's address, an attacker can use fake data to respond to that request telling it to connect to a device they have control over.

MITM Attack Techniques
Sniffing

An attacker can use a packet capturing tool to capture data packets in the network. Using wireless devices that can be configured to monitoring mode will allow that attacker to sniff out packets send to hosts within the network.

Packet Injection

The monitoring mode can also be used to insert malicious data packets into the communication stream. These packets will blend with the valid data which will make them part of the communication although these are malicious in nature. Sniffing is usually the prerequisite to packet injection as the hacker tries to determined how to craft the malicious packets and when to send them.

SSL Stripping

HTTPS encrypts data, which is why it's commonly used to protect against DNS or ARP spoofing. But attackers can intercept the packets and modify the HTTPS-based request to redirect it to the HTTP equivalent endpoint. Communication is then done in plain text so sensitive information can easily be captured.

Preventing MITM Attacks
Virtual Private Network or VPN

To protect sensitive information in a LAN or local area network, a secure environment can be created using a VPN. A subnet is created for secure communication by using key-based encryption. Even if the attacker was able to connect to the network, they won't be able to decrypt the traffic.

Strong Access Point Encryption

When a strong encryption mechanism is implemented on your wireless access points, it can prevent unwanted users from getting into the network even though they are within the wireless network range. An attacker can use a brute-force attack if the encryption mechanism is weak and then implement a MITM attack.

Public Key Pair Based Authentication

MITM attacks often involve spoofing in one way or another. Public key pair based authentication such as RSA is commonly used to ensure that devices are communicating with other devices securely.

Chapter 7. Malware Attacks

A malware attack requires that malicious software be run on the victim's system to launch unauthorized actions. The malware (or virus) encompasses a lot of attack types such as spyware, command and control, ransomware, and more.

Examining Malware Attacks

Malware is usually designed using these main aspects:

- Objective – what is it designed to do?

- Delivery – how will it be delivered to the victim?

- Concealment – how will it avoid detection?

Objectives

There is always an objective behind each malware ever developed. Here are the most common objectives of malware:

Extracting Information

Stealing payment information, credentials, data, etc. is probably the most common objective in a cybercrime. Malware designed for this activity can be extremely damaging to an individual, business, or government if they fall victim to this attack.

Disrupting Operations

Malware can also be designed to disrupt the normal operations of the target. The level of disruption may vary depending on the capability of the malware and the vulnerabilities in a system. It can be as simple as corrupting files, making systems unusable, or initiating a self-destruct action. Infected systems can also be hijacked to take part in large scale DDoS attacks.

Demanding Payment

Some malware is designed to specifically extort money. Scareware uses threats that can't really be carried out to 'scare' victims into paying money. Ransomware can 'kidnap' data by encrypting it making it unusable unless the victim pays up. Most ransomware attackers demand a virtual currency such as Bitcoin for payment.

Malware Attack Vectors

Vectors are the methods of malware delivery and here are the three main types.

- Trojan Horse. This malware will appear to be a valid software (e.g. a useful application, a game, etc.) but in reality, it's a delivery mechanism. A Trojan horse needs to be executed on a target to infect the system.

- Virus. This malware propagates itself by infecting other files or applications and sometimes even parts of an operating system through code injection. This propagating behavior of a virus differentiates it from a Trojan horse because the latter was particularly developed to infect one application and does not infect others.

- Worm. This malware not only propagates itself inside a single system but also infects others, too. Trojan horses and viruses are often localized to a single system but the worm infects other targets actively even without user interaction.

Malware has been found to use different attack vectors throughout the years. While some are academic, many of these vectors are very effective. The attack vectors mostly occur via electronic communications such as a compromised website, vulnerable network service, text, or email. It can also be delivered using physical media such as CD/DVD, USB thumb drives, etc.

Preventing Malware Attacks

The following tips can be used to prevent malware attacks or mitigate the damage incurred after an attack.

User Education

Users should be trained on the best practices on avoiding malware such as not inserting unknown media or downloading/installing unknown software into their systems. Identifying potential malware such as unexpected processes or applications running inside their systems or phishing emails should also be part of their training. Running unannounced cybersecurity drills like simulated phishing attacks can keep users observant and aware.

Use Antivirus

An antivirus solution can detect and also remove malware in a system. Some can even mitigate and monitor potential malware activity or installation. Just make sure it's updated with the latest signatures or definitions from the vendor.

Secure the Network

The organization's network should only be accessible to those who are authorized to do so it's a good idea to keep it secure. There are technologies and methodologies that can be implemented to fortify the security of your networks such as firewalls, and intrusion prevention/detection systems. These tools help reduce the surface of attack that can be exploited by potential attackers. Some organizations even implement isolation or 'air gapping'.

Perform Security Audits on Your Website

Your organization's websites should be regularly scanned for vulnerabilities such as application/service/server misconfiguration, or known software bugs and check if malware has been installed. These keep the visitors, customers, employees, and the organization secure.

Create Regular Backups

If you have a regular backup that you keep current and off-site, you can quickly recover from a ransomware attack or a destructive virus, instead of facing costly data loss or downtime. Backups should be verified if running as scheduled and are usable if ever data restoration is required. Outdated backups hold less value than the later ones, and backups that can't be restored are useless.

Attacks can happen in different ways and malware can take different forms. With process improvements and good planning including user education, you can build a solid defense against malware attacks.

Chapter 8. Denial-of-Service Attacks

Denial-of-service or DoS attacks work by preventing or disrupting valid users from accessing applications, websites, or other resources. DoS attacks have been used by cybercriminals in extorting money, by activists to state their ideals, and state actors to get back at their adversaries.

The effect of DoS attacks can vary widely. A smartphone rebooting due to a deluge of text messages might be a little inconvenient for the user while an attack on an online business' website preventing buyers from accessing it can cost a lot of money. As more systems get connected, DoS attack has become an even more serious threat to organizations, businesses, and governments.

Types of DoS Attacks

Through the years, DoS attacks have grown to include a number of mechanisms and vectors

Distributed Denial-of-Service or DDoS

DoS attacks originally involved just one system attacking another and it can still be done in that fashion. Most modern-day DoS attacks, however, involve a lot of systems that are being controlled by an attacker to simultaneously attack a target. This is called a distributed denial-of-service attack and is the method of choice for attackers when carrying out other DoS attack types.

Network-Targeted DoS

In this type of attack, the attacker will try to flood the connection and use up the bandwidth so that legitimate traffic between the targeted systems is disrupted that's why it's also called 'bandwidth consumption attack'. Attackers may also use distributed reflection denial-of-service or DRDoS which tricks unwitting systems into helping with the attack which floods the target system with network traffic. During the attack, legitimate systems and users will have difficulty accessing systems that they normally have access to.

Another variation of the Network-Targeted DoS requires bringing down or altering the network by targeting the network devices (wireless access points, routers, switches, etc.) disallowing traffic to flow regularly to and from the devices. This leads to a similar DoS effect but there is no flooding involved.

System-Targeted Denial-of-Service

This attack focuses on reducing the usability of systems. A common vector in system-targeted denial-of-service is depleting the resource of a system (e.g. disk space, CPU, memory, etc.) to the point that normal operations of the target is crippled. SYN flooding is a good example of this attack. It uses up the incoming network connections of a system disallowing access from other systems and users. A system-targeted denial-of-service attack's result can be a minor slowdown or disruption or it can crash the whole system. Although uncommon, there are even attacks that may require a physical repair of the system or outright replacement.

Application-Targeted Denial-of-Service

This is another popular vector for the DoS attack wherein the application itself is the target. What makes it hard to defend against is that it usually uses existing, normal behavior of the software or application in order to create a DoS scenario. Some examples are locking out users from applications or sending requests that put stress on an essential part of the application (e.g. central database) until users are unable to use or access the application as expected or intended. Application-targeted attacks may also rely on existing vulnerabilities in the application itself like triggering error conditions that will crash the application, or gaining direct access to the system to further intensify the DoS attack.

Controlling DoS Attacks

Here are some suggestions that you should consider in order to reduce the surface of attack on your organization or minimize the damaging effects of DoS attacks.

Review the application's architecture and its implementation

Never allow user actions in a system that may deplete its resources or overconsume its components. Check resources available online for best-practice suggestions on how to do this.

Monitoring and Alerting

The following should be monitored for abnormal behavior:

- Network traffic. Unexpected and abnormally high network utilization might be a sign of a network-target DoS attack. Analyze the type of traffic as well as the origin for additional insight.

- System health. Identify and prevent system-targeted DoS attacks by monitoring the usage of system resources such as CPU, storage, and memory. Set thresholds that will alert you when there's unexplained high utilization of these resources.

- Application health. Application components should be frequently checked if they are still performing assigned tasks within the expected timeframe. Frequent breaching of this threshold might indicate an application-targeted DoS attack.

Vendors of datacenter and cloud systems usually also offer monitoring solutions for their products. Ask if the provider can provide a demo to see if their monitoring and/or alerting solutions fit your system requirements.

Chapter 9. Spear Phishing Attacks

Spear phishing is a type of phishing attack targeting only a particular group or recipient by crafting a targeted and detailed email. Because of the information required by the attack, the attacker will need to research the target and gather important details to include in the email to make it look like it's coming from a legitimate sender. Like other phishing attack types, the success of the attack lies in the hope that the target falls into the trap and click a link, download a malicious payload, or initiating an action like transferring money.

Spear phishing attacks usually target one organization at a time, or just a specific team in an organization. This type of attack can also get more granular and focus on the biggest targets such as senior managers or C-level executives. This is called whaling and will be discussed in detail on another chapter.

Just like catching fish in real life, an attacker should cast a wide net when sending a phishing email hoping to make a catch in the process. That's why the attack is often done by sending spam mails coming from a legitimate source hoping that an unwitting recipient would launch an attachment or click a link so the perpetrator can obtain valuable credentials or sensitive information.

Phishing attacks have been around for so long because they are effective, lucrative, and cheap. But as cybersecurity evolves, flagging common phishing strategies have become easier. User education also ensures that even if that phishing email reaches the intended destination, users won't be fooled.

This is the reason for these new phishing tactics that are made to be more believable. Casting a wide net is giving way to strategies that are focused on using authentic details to make the phishing email look legitimate. Thus, spear fishing was born.

The Usual Target

Enterprises usually publish their company data online and this information could be mined by attackers without looking suspicious. This is what makes these large companies susceptible to a spear phishing attack. These company websites contain a lot of data such as events, customers, key company personnel, business-specific jargon and technical details, and even the applications being used. By scanning social networks such LinkedIn, Twitter, and Facebook, attackers can find details of where a person has worked, or currently works. Attackers can then have a view of the corporate hierarchy using this goldmine of data.

A spear phishing email usually contains a sprinkling of these details that are available online such as terms, places, or names which can lend it sufficient validity for a savvy recipient to be convinced and launch a malicious link. The link may be redirected to a specially designed website that can gather sensitive credentials which then allows the attacker to penetrate the organization's internal network and steal customer data or intellectual property.

By figuring out how the internal email addresses of a company is structured, for example, names of key personnel (gathered through LinkedIn), key customer identities (usually found in corporate blogs), and who the sales head is (on the 'about us" page), the perpetrator is able to draft a convincing email to the whole account management team, which looks like it's coming from the sales head, regarding an important issue they have with a big customer. The email could state that a memo located in the corporate intranet needs to be reviewed by the recipients. This link will look very much like the corporate portal but actually, it's a decoy designed to gather usernames and passwords. Financial departments are usually targeted by spear phishing attacks during the tax preparation season which may look like it's coming from the organization's CFO or CEO requiring the recipients to review an important W2 paperwork.

Preventing Spear Phishing Attacks

The common strategies used in generic phishing attacks could also be used to defend against spear phishing. It can't be reiterated enough that users should never click a link embedded in emails as this is the launching pad for these attacks. Spear phishing is a version of the old phishing tactics that have evolved so businesses need to ensure that this is mention in the policies and that they're implementing specific solutions to educate employees about this particular type of phishing attack.

Other tips that an organization may consider in defending against spear phishing include:

- Remind users to always inspect the emails they receive if those contain unsolicited links or attachments. Reminders on the dangers of spear phishing may also be sent to all employees during certain times of the year such as tax season or after a big company announcement.

- Deploy both commercial and open-source threat intelligence solutions to actively track spear phishing campaigns and block them in real time.

- All employees should undergo periodic awareness training programs to ensure that they keep best security practices.

- Create a venue for reporting suspected phishing messages and provide access to all employees. This way, your team will be notified immediately if there is an ongoing spear phishing attack on the organization.

Don't settle for just 'classroom training' in your campaign against phishing attacks. Simulate phishing scenarios by sending convincing but harmless spear phishing emails to the employees. If your users fall for this attempt, they'll have first-hand knowledge of how effective spear phishing campaigns can be and you can do this while keeping business data safe. The employees are your front liners against phishing attacks and the organization can benefit the most when users are trained properly and regularly

Chapter 10. Whaling Phishing Attacks

When a spear phishing attack is targeting high-profile personnel such as executives, it's colloquially called whaling because of the huge catch involved if the attack is successful. Attackers are aware that these high-level employees are more email savvy and can point out usual spam strategies because they may have undergone extensive training on security awareness and security teams are more protective of these people. So to increase the chance of success, attackers look beyond the old strategies and employ targeted and more sophisticated methods.

As with other phishing attacks, a whaling attempt on a high-profile user also relies on convincing the target and this is usually done with a sense of urgency to make the email more compelling. Usual outcomes usually involve coercing the target to take an action such as transferring money or open an attachment or click a link that redirects the target to a believable corporate portal or install malware. The most common goal of these attackers is to capture personal and sensitive information, such as user credentials, that will give them access to customer data, intellectual property, or information that they can sell on black markets.

Because of increasing public awareness on common phishing strategies, attackers are changing the approach by focusing on big targets and crafting emails with details enough to convince the recipient of the email's authenticity, compelling them to act. This is what whaling is all about.

The usual targets of whaling such as C-level executives or media spokespersons usually have their information published on the corporate website available for the public to see and attackers to exploit. These senior employees usually have high-level access to internal data compared to the common employee. Some might even have administrative rights to company systems. The target pool for whaling might be small because there are less people at the top of the corporate ladder but the payout can be lucrative.

Whaling Attack Examples

Successful whaling attacks in the past have been done using tactics that are pretty much similar to the usual phishing campaigns. The main difference is that these messages are crafted so that they seem urgent and even potentially disastrous in order to compel the recipients to immediately take action without considering best security practices. Attackers are aware that the target won't be convinced by a simple deadline reminder or even a superior's stern email. To make the scenario more compelling, they prey on the target's fears such as reputational harm or legal action.

In one successful whaling attack, executives from different industries fell for an email which contained accurate personal details and the organizations they work for coming from a Unites States District Court asking them to appear before a jury due to a civil case. The email contained a link the purported subpoena, but when clicked, recipients were infected with a malware.

Whaling Defense

The usual advice for preventing and protecting against phishing attacks still apply to whaling. That is, users, no matter the stature in the company, should beware of opening attachments or clicking links contained in emails since any kind of phishing attack still need action from the user in order to be successful.

Similar with spear phishing, organizations should employ tools to harden their defenses and also train potential whaling targets on best practices against whaling-specific attacks.

The organization should first recognize the information provided by public-facing employees about company executives. Details that are easily gathered through sites such as social may contain anything from hometowns to birthdays, to favorite sports or hobbies, can be used by attackers to make the email more believable. Attackers may also use major public events for added legitimacy so spokespersons or executives should be told to be particularly wary of the emails they receive during and after such events.

Next, a 'trust but verify' email culture should be fostered in the organization. All employees need to verify the authenticity of unexpected and urgent messages via a different communication channel such as texting or calling, or talking in person with the sender. Senior management and executives should lead by example with this practice.

Most important of them all and this can't be repeated enough, a phishing awareness program should be implemented and this should include content that are targeted for public-facing employees and senior management about the whaling related emails they might receive. The program should be multi-faceted and should not just teach basic principles but put the employees' knowledge to the test. Simulated whaling attacks should be done on potential targets to hone their skills in recognizing the attempt.

Chapter 11. Dictionary and Brute-force Attacks

In a dictionary and brute-force attack, the attacker attempts to log in using a user's account and trying out each possible password or passphrase until it's successful.

Attackers know that the front door is still the easiest way for an attack on a system and there's always a way to access it and that is through logging in. If you know the correct credentials to access a system, you will be able to log in normally and since maybe you don't need to try multiple times, there would be no suspicious access attempts logged or you don't trigger an intrusion-detection-system or IDS alert. Life can be much easier if you a system administrator's credentials. Attackers may not have this information at hand so they need to employ techniques such dictionary and brute-force attacks to get into the system.

Attackers usually start by looking for a potential victim's email address or domain together with the passwords that can be gathered from compromised websites. Password reuse is a common mistake made by people logging into different sites and using the same email account and password on both private (email or corporate intranet) and public (social media or site memberships) domains. Knowing this, an attacker can try if the dumped user account and password is still valid. In the case of savvy users, they often use different email accounts and passwords on different sites and systems. The attacker must now use a different approach and that is through dictionary and brute-force attacks.

Dictionary Attacks

In this type of attack, a wordlist is used containing commonly used words with the attacker hoping that the password will match one of those words. Dictionary attacks work very well on simple passwords such as 'airplanes' or 'computer'. These wordlists may also contain commonly used passwords such as 'password', 'iloveyou', 'letmein, and '12345678'. Modern systems prevent the use of simple passwords by requiring more complex ones containing numbers, special characters, and capital letters, or those that are not usually found in wordlists.

Brute-Force Attacks

In a brute-force attack, the attacker uses a tool designed to try each combination of numbers and letters, expecting that the password will be eventually guessed. If the attacker is aware that passwords for the target organization is checked for complexity and should include symbols or special characters, those are added in the combination, too. No matter the how complex or strong the password is, brute-force attacks can crack it but it might take a long time to do so.

It takes less than a minute to guess a short password like a 4-digit PIN. For six characters, it might take an hour. Using a combination of letters, numbers, and symbols, the crack attempt will take days. Each character added to the password requires more time for a brute-force attack to guess it. Lengthy and strong passwords might take months to be guessed. Eventually though, the password will be discovered after some time and with sufficient computing power.

Dictionary and Brute-Force Attack Defense

Although not impossible, using complex and uncommon passwords will require more time and might deter an attacker. For even more effective measures against these kinds of attacks, you might consider these

Slowing down login attempts

It's a simple countermeasure but can be very effective. For example, you can delay subsequent login attempts by a mere 0.1 seconds. This minimal delay won't be noticed by the users but attackers using dictionary and brute-force attacks will take a much longer time to guess the password especially if attempts can't be made in parallel.

Locking accounts

A much better approach against these kinds of attack is to lock accounts if users are unable to login after a number of attempts. Most websites have additional protection when they detect repeated password attempts. An iPhone, for example, self-destructs after 10 failed login tries.

Refreshing passwords

Modern systems can be configured that users' passwords be changed periodically. Some environments might require a password change every 30 days and some do it every 90 days. The reason behind this method is that an attacker using dictionary and brute-force attack will need weeks to crack a complex password. If the password has been changed while the attack is still ongoing, the attack should start again from the beginning. However, many users confess using sequential passwords such 'airplanes2018', 'airplanes2019', and so on which are easier to crack.

Monitoring for abnormal behavior

A security savvy organization might use a tool to monitor anomalies during the login process like repeated login tries or logins from devices or locations that are not registered to the system. The security team will then be able to detect and lock an account, block the device's IP address, contact the user, or do further research on the hacker's activity.

Dictionary and brute-force attacks are very effective against simple systems that's why these are very common in small businesses. For complex environments, however, these attacks can only be successful when the login attempts can be blended into normal operations, or be used on cracking password hashes from a password database. Knowing how these attacks work should be a part of a security professional's arsenal.

Chapter 12. Securing the Infrastructure

The digital world is becoming increasingly connected that it's no longer practical for infrastructure managers and owners to remain unfazed by evolving cyber threats. An integrated cyber defense that involves securing physical infrastructure must be built up, and fast.

In a recent report by The BBC, researchers discovered troubling major security vulnerabilities affecting traffic monitoring, radiation detection, and flood defenses – in infrastructures located in major cities in Europe and the US. Of those vulnerabilities, almost ten are categorized as critical, which would mean that a cyberattack targeting these systems would debilitate important infrastructures which include water treatment facilities, power grids, and similar large-scale systems.

It's the stuff movies are made of, the city loses electricity, the people panic, planes are grounded, and the roads get clogged. Communicating with the frightened public or coordinating rescue efforts seem almost impossible. Although scenarios such as this seem far-fetched, they are real.

In 2015, hackers attacked Ukraine's power grid and in the following hours, hundreds of thousands of homes and offices were left with no power. Unfortunately, this and other similar stories rarely reach the masses so there's very little pressure on cybersecurity decision-makers and attackers are generally ignored.

As the world continues to be more and more connected, the number as well the severity of these cyberattacks will only continue to exponentially grow. An estimate from Gartner states that more than 20 billion devices will be connected via the Internet by 2020, and a large number of this will be used for infrastructure control and monitoring. The proliferation of connected devices might mean efficiency and productivity gains but it also exposes infrastructure systems, which were previously unreachable, to attacks from malicious groups.

Financiers, builders, planners, and owners invest a lot of resources in mitigating risks to infrastructure assets but very rarely do they turn the same attention to anticipating potential cyberattacks.

There are various reasons why cybersecurity might be taken for granted. The most common one is the belief that the technology used to secure physical infrastructures is different from those used in other industries. Actually, it's not. Although technology solutions continue to evolve in operating infrastructures, these solutions are still running on the same operating systems also used by other sectors.

Also, infrastructure managers believe that they should hire cybersecurity professionals that are industry-specific. Although industry-specific expertise can be beneficial, it's not really essential since the tools used in cybersecurity are pretty much the same, no matter what the business is. If operators and owners focus on hiring specialized talent, it will delay any cybersecurity program they might have in line.

Currently, the infrastructure industry still needs to catch up when it comes to cybersecurity. To achieve this goal, organizations and cities must pool up their resources and integrate their defenses. They need to recruit talent and come up with a cybersecurity program. Also, they need to ensure that infrastructures are resilient to cyberattacks as more processes and procedures are getting digitized.

Chapter 13. Securing Your Local Network

A Local Area Network or LAN is a type of network connecting computers and other devices within a limited area such as an office building, a computer laboratory, a school, or a house. Compared to Wide Area Networks or WANs which span larger distances, LANs usually allow very high data transfer rates.

The Local Area Network can be further classified into wired and wireless network devices. Although securing both types is basically the same, there are also some differences.

Securing a Wired Network

With more and more offices adopting a 'work anywhere' environment, wired networks seem to have taken a back seat. But a recent surge in threats coming from inside the network and social engineering attacks seeking access to the local network, securing the local wired network should not be taken for granted.

Mapping and Auditing

If it hasn't been done recently, mapping and auditing the network is an activity that needs to be scheduled regularly. A network administrator should always have a detailed understanding of the whole network infrastructure which includes the brand and model, basic configuration, and location of firewalls, switches, routers, wireless access points, and Ethernet ports and cabling. There should be an updated documentation on what computers, servers, printers, and other networked devices are connected, where these devices are connected, and the connectivity patch of each device throughout the network.

During mapping and auditing, some security vulnerabilities might be discovered or ways on how reliability, performance, and security can be further enhanced. Physical security threats or an incorrectly configured firewall may also be discovered during this assessment.

For small networks that involve only a few network components and less than a dozen computers, mapping and auditing can be done manually and the results written or printed on paper. Mapping and auditing larger networks might require a specialized program that can be used to scan the entire network and produce a logical network map which can be printed later.

Updating the Network

Once the mapping and auditing have been completed, a deeper dive into the network components should be considered. Check for software or firmware updates that are available for all the network components. This can usually be done by checking the current version and comparing it with what's available on the vendors' support website.

Ensuring that default passwords have been changed is also an important part of keeping the network updated as well as checking for security functionality and features that are not being used, and reviewing the current settings for any configuration that may render the device insecure.

The next objects that should be checked are the computers and other devices currently connected to the local network. Basic things that should be considered are that drivers and OS are updated, personal firewalls are properly configured and active, strong passwords are set, and that antivirus software is updated and working.

Securing the Network Physically

This is often minimized or overlooked, but a network's physical security is as crucial as a firewall facing the Internet. Just as the network needs to be protected from viruses, bots, and hackers, it needs to be safeguarded from local threats, too.

Without sound physical security of the network and the building itself, a nearby perpetrator or an employee with malicious intent can take advantage of the existing vulnerabilities. For example, the attacker can use an open port in an Ethernet switch to plug in a wireless router which gives access to anyone nearby without being physically connected to the network. If that particular Ethernet port was disabled or hidden, the attack wouldn't have succeeded.

Ensuring that there is good building security in place helps in preventing outsiders from getting into the premises. Wiring closets and other areas where network components are located should be physically secured from unauthorized users and that includes both the employees and the public.

Use cabinet and door locks to security network components to prevent unauthorized access and confirm that Ethernet cables are not exposed in plain sight and aren't physically accessible. The same applies to wireless access points. Disable Ethernet ports that are not in use using the switch's or router's configuration, especially if these devices are in areas exposed to the public.

Filtering MAC Addresses

A major security issue with wired networks is the lack of encryption methods or quick authentication. Anyone can plug in a device into an available and enabled Ethernet port and be able to access the network. Wireless networks can easily be secured using authentication and encryption protocols.

This is where MAC address filtering comes in. Using this method, only devices which are listed in the MAC address filter will be allowed access to the network.

Although it's possible for a determined hacker to bypass MAC address filtering, it can still be considered as additional security layer. It might not completely stop the hacker but it can stop an employee from creating a serious security hole such as allowing a visitor to connect to the network through an open Ethernet port.

MAC address filtering allows more control over the devices that can connect to the network but the list should be updated and checked on a regular basis.

Segregating Network Traffic Using VLANs

VLANs are used to segment a network into virtual networks. It's usually used to group Ethernet ports, users, and wireless access points among the virtual networks.

Another use of VLANs is segregating the network by the type of traffic (e.g. DMZ, SAN, VoIP, or general access) for design or performance reasons or types of users (e.g. guests, employees, management) for security reasons.

VLANs are particularly useful in dynamic assignments. For example, a user can plug in a computer anywhere within the network or through Wi-Fi and be automatically assigned to the proper VLAN. This is achieved through MAC address tagging or using 801.1X authentication as a more secure option.

To implement VLANs, the switches and routers must support it. Check for IEEE 802.1Q support in the manual or specification sheets of the product. Advanced wireless access points support both multiple SSIDs and VLAN tagging allowing multiple virtual WLANs to be assigned to particular VLANs.

Implementing 802.1X Authentication

Encryption and authentication in wired networks are usually ignored because of complexity reasons. Although it's best practice to encrypt wireless network connections, the same should also be applied wired ones. Without it, a hacker who's able to plug into the network will be able to send and receive data and there's nothing to stop them.

Implementing 802.1X authentication won't encrypt Ethernet traffic but it can stop perpetrators from sending data over the network or access resources until a valid login credential has been provided. This authentication protocol can be implemented in wireless networks as well so enterprise-level WPA2 security with AES encryption can be used instead of the less secure personal-level security of WPA2. And as previously mentioned, 802.1X can be used VLAN dynamic assignments.

A Remote Authentication Dial-In User Service or RADIUS server is required to implement 802.1X authentication. The RADIUS hosts the user database and is used to authorize or deny access to the network. Windows Server already has a built-in RADIUS server as well as the Network Policy Server or NPS role. There are also standalone RADIUS servers available.

Encrypting Select Machines Using VPN

Securing network traffic requires encryption. Even with 802.1X authentication and VLANs implemented, a hacker can still eavesdrop on the local network and capture unencrypted data traffic that may contain sensitive data such as documents, emails, and even usernames and passwords.

Although it's possible to encrypt all traffic, an analysis of the network should be done first. It might be more practical to encrypt selected communications that are considered sensitive but unencrypted using SSL or HTTPS. Sensitive traffic can also be passed through standard VPN which can be configured to be enabled when sensitive communication is required or forced to be always enabled.

Encrypting the Entire Network

As previously mentioned, it's possible to encrypt the entire network and one option would be to use IPSec. A Windows Server machine can be configured as an IPSec server and that same OS also natively supports the required client capability. However, encrypting the entire network can be an overhead burden because of the processing power needed to encrypt and decrypt data. This can make effective throughput rates to drop dramatically. To reduce overhead and latency, there are network encryption solutions available that use Layer 2 and not Layer 3 encryption.

Securing a Wireless Network

A lot of money is put into securing local networks and keeping unauthorized users off, but wireless access points, if not secured, can provide a convenient channel for hackers to get in.

That's mainly because wireless signal broadcasts can extend beyond the walls of homes or buildings and even reach the streets. This is an enticing scenario for hackers. It's the reason why drive-by hacking or wardriving is among the favorite pastimes of cybercriminals.

Many companies openly allow and sometimes even encourage their employees to connect wirelessly to the network using mobile devices such as laptops, smartphones, or tablets. This makes turning off Wi-Fi access impractical.

This also applies to residential broadband users who have guests frequently coming over to whom they want to share their

Internet connection. This makes securing the wireless network important and here are some tips to do it.

Using Stronger Encryption

There are still Wi-Fi access points using the old Wired Equivalent Privacy or WEP standard of protection. This protection is practically broken and easy to breach. It will only take a hacker a few minutes to break into a wireless network protected by WEP using a hacking tool such as Aircrack-ng.

To keep these intruders out, it's important to use a stronger encryption protocol such as Wi-Fi Protected Access or WPA or the more secure WPA2 standard.

For some companies, it might not be practical to implement WPA using a pre-shared key. With WPA, all users will use the same password Wi-Fi password to connect. This information can easily be passed to an unauthorized person through social engineering methods. The network security is then dependent on employees not sharing this password with others outside the organization. The Wi-Fi password also needs to be changed whenever an employee has left the company.

There are Wi-Fi routers that have Wireless Protect Setup or WPS built-in. This feature provides a simple way to connect wireless devices to a network protected with WPA. This setup, however, is easy to exploit allowing hackers to retrieve the WPA password. To prevent this, WPS should be disabled in the router's configuration settings.

Larger organizations usually implement enterprise-level WPA wherein employees use their own domain usernames and passwords to access the Wi-Fi network. This setup is easier to manage and password don't need to be changed when employees leave. The resigned employee's account just needs to be disabled. To implement this, a RADIUS server needs to be set up.

Using Secure WPA Passwords

If WPA via pre-shared key needs to be implemented, the password used should be long, random, and composed of a combination of letters (capital and small), numbers, and special characters. Better yet, use a passphrase instead of a password so cracking via brute-force attack will be difficult.

Setting up wireless access points and routers might be easy using the default settings because the default administrator name and administrator password are usually printed on the device itself which allows easy access and setup. Hackers maintain a database of default device administrator names and passwords which they use when they try to breach the network. Ensure that default passwords and usernames are changed after the device has been set up.

One way to test the WPA protected network's security is by using a tool called the CloudCracker service. This utility will attempt to sniff out or capture data wirelessly using a laptop that is within the range of the wireless network then try to extract the password. The tool gives a report when the password has been cracked but the password itself is not revealed.

Checking for Rogue Access Points

A rogue wireless access point is a critical security risk. This is not an official access point but one that an employee may have brought in maybe because it's hard to get a good network signal in their area) or by hackers who were able to get inside the business premises, plug in the device into an open Ethernet port, and hide it.

There's no way to control or configure a rogue access point. It could be set up to broadcast the wireless network identifier or SSID and allow connection without requiring a Wi-Fi password.

Detecting rogue access points requires scanning the offices in the company and the nearby areas using a tool such as airodump-ng or Vistumbler. These applications sniff the wireless network to detect traffic being transferred to and from rogue access points and determine where they may be located.

Providing a Separate Network for Visitors

If the organization wants to allow guests to access the corporate Wi-Fi, a guest network separate from the company's network can be provided. Visitors can then access the Internet but they won't be able to access the company's internal network. This secures the local network and prevents unauthorized devices from infecting the network with malware.

One way this can be implemented is through an Internet connection that is separate from the one used in the internal network. Most business-grade and newer consumer Wi-Fi routers are capable of running multiple Wi-Fi networks. One can be configured for the main corporate network and the other for guests.

WPA protection should be enabled on the guest network instead of leaving it open and there are a couple of important reasons behind it. One is to achieve some control over who uses the guest Wi-Fi network. The password can be provided to the guests upon request and changed frequently to prevent the number of people knowing the password from going too large. The other is to protect the visitors from other people who are also connected to the guest network who might attempt to snoop on the traffic and capture sensitive data. Although guests are connected via the same WPA password, data is encrypted individually using different session keys.

Hiding the Network Name

The Service Set Identifier or SSID is the name of the wireless network and is being broadcast by the Wi-Fi access point by default so that users can easily find and connect to it. It's possible to 'hide' the SSID so that only people who know the network name can connect.

This makes sense to implement in a company where the employees know the SSID of the Wi-Fi network so there's no use for it to be broadcast and be discovered by anyone else passing by or within the area.

Hiding the SSID should not be the only measure taken in securing the Wi-Fi network. Hackers can still use Wi-Fi scanning tools to detect hidden networks. Still, hiding the network provides another security layer that perpetrators must circumvent.

Using a Firewall

Hardware firewalls can act as the first layer of security against attacks from the outside. Most modern routers already have firewalls built-in which can check incoming and outgoing data, and block suspicious activities. These devices do a decent job of protecting the internal network even at default settings.

Most firewalls utilize packet filtering which involves looking at packet headers to determine the source address and the destination. This information is then compared to predefined rules that decide if the packet is legitimate or malicious in nature, and also if it should be allowed or discarded.

Software firewalls are usually configured on laptops or desktops and they have the advantage of having a better vantage point on the traffic passing through. The firewall will know the applications that are in use and can block or allow data to be sent or received in addition to where data is going and which ports are used.

Software firewalls usually ask the user what should be done if it doesn't recognize a program before it allows or blocks traffic.

Enabling MAC Filtering

The same with wired networks, wireless networks can be further secured by allowing only those devices whose MAC addresses belong to a whitelist. This way, only authorized devices will have access to the corporate Wi-Fi connection. Although there may be ways to circumvent this like MAC address spoofing, filtering still adds another layer of obstacle for would-be hackers.

Using a VPN

A Virtual Private Network or VPN helps keep users stay secure and safe while connected via a public network by keeping private stuff private. It uses encryption to keep information hidden from eavesdroppers. In theory, a hacker could get inside the network but still unable to inflict any damage or steal data as long as VPN is implemented.

Chapter 14. Securing the Perimeter

Attackers are constantly targeting data centers. Hacks are being uncovered on a daily basis wherein millions of identities are stolen, websites are brought down, cash is ripped off from financial systems, and sensitive information is made public.

This gives the impression that the IT guys whom employees have trusted for years to protect their data can no longer do their jobs as expected. That might be an unfair assessment, though.

So, what's happening? According to security surveys over the past few decades, the volume and size of cyberattacks have grown exponentially. This includes the number of probable attack vectors. Imagine a fortified city being attacked from the inside by insurgents and the officials don't want the gates to be closed because of the effect on trade and economy.

That's how security professionals look at the situation from the perspective of the data center. Business managers have learned about the benefits of the cloud and they want in, now. These people won't stand and wait for internally developed systems or for applications to be approved by the IT department.

There are thousands of cloud applications out there and it's impossible to block all of them. To make it more difficult, most of the data these security professionals are trying to protect is being shared via applications through a channel that is not physically connected to the organization's network perimeter security device. They are accessing important data store in the cloud directly from public places like coffee shops and airports.

Even the most locked-down firewall hosting a list of blocked applications is useless if the app's user is mobile or remote.

Anti-virus applications are also struggling to counteract today's threats.

New Perimeter

Traditionally, perimeter defense meant controlling traffic that flows in and out of the data center network. According to best practices, a layered set of additional defenses should be implemented.

In addition to a router the external and internal networks, a firewall should be set up to protect the perimeter. The firewall filters out unknown or potentially dangerous traffic using a set of rules that assess the captured data and decide if it constitutes a threat. Intrusion prevention or intrusion detection systems may also be deployed which monitors traffic for suspicious activities after it passes through a firewall.

Implementing multiple layers of controls that complement each other is a result of an effective security strategy. Potential intruders, in order to gain access to the internal network, must circumvent all of these security tools. But as attackers and attacks have gotten more and more sophisticated, perimeter defense alone may not be enough. Businesses need to develop AI-enhanced network monitoring, incident response, and threat detection capabilities as well.

Although antivirus applications, network perimeter security appliances, and firewalls may have lost a bit of potency due to the complexity of modern attacks, organizations should not abandon them. These systems can still be used to counteract direct attacks. Firewalls still play an important role in securing the perimeter but what requires more attention nowadays is the 'human firewall'. The security perimeter now includes all devices and all employees.

We have discussed how easy it is to do a phishing attack through email. Cybersecurity is not just about technology, it's about people, too. That's why training plays a huge role in cyberattack prevention.

In a recent phishing attack on a northeastern seaboard company, the data center people were left scrambling for days. The attack began when an employee opened a malicious link embedded in an email that was cleverly and meticulously engineered. That action lets attackers gain access to the organization's address books. In a few minutes, employees got emails from other employees asking them to open a fax document that was attached. Understandably, many opened the document which rapidly spread the infection leading to several systems being made unavailable or compromised.

Incidents such as this emphasize the importance of employee training as part of the security arsenal of every data center. According to a security survey, organizations that train their employees spend up to 76% less on cybersecurity incidents compared to organizations that don't train their people. The savings, according to the survey, amounted to around half a million dollars annually.

It's important, then, to safeguard the data center perimeter at all gates. These include the network edge, the corporate firewall, and outward to the cloud and mobile applications, as well as inward to every device and every employee in the organization. This can be a very daunting task for security professionals. It's like protecting the president on his visit to the Bronx. The only seemingly viable option is to put the area on lockdown and deploy Secret Service staff, drones, and jet fighters. This level of protection is not viable for most data centers.

Fortunately, there might not be a need to. Security experts believe that it's essential to prioritize not only with regards to cost but also to increase the effectiveness of measures against cyberattacks. It's not necessary to protect the whole infrastructure, just safeguard what is vital to the organization.

Advocating Threat Intelligence

Security costs can be contained by putting most of the effort and resources in protecting the 'crown jewels' of the data center. But there's a way to make the task easier through implementing intelligence and analytics techniques.

There are cutting-edge network analytics and forensics tools already available that can make incident management as well as response management more efficient by providing essential information when an attack happens. Analytics is now getting the 'big data' treatment. These tools can take care of the 'heavy lifting' tasks during a cyberattack.

The goal of these tools is to determine if something is behaving abnormally in the network. An attack usually entails activities that are not normally happening in the network like machines talking to other machines that they don't usually communicate with. With a context of which machines should be doing particular activities, combined with the information on the protocols, ports, and hosts they normally interact with, it's easy to determine when something is off.

If one of the machines in the network is doing something different than it normally does, the system alerts the data center management team. The security professional can then check if it's a real threat or not. McAfee, RSA, and Symantec have begun to develop similar tools. High-speed and real-time advanced analytics is the best solution if high-level resilience is required.

Threat intelligence is also something that should be advocated across all businesses and industries. Information sharing on attempted attacks among these organizations will level the playing field. These attackers are organized and they're helping each other in their attacks. The same thing should happen between organizations in the fight against cybercrime.

Data centers should no longer be acting as though they are isolated. The goal should be to pool their resources to form a united front in defending against these perpetrators.

Management and Response

Most data centers focus mainly on quick response to immediate threats. Although important, it's not a viable long-term approach. Datacenter personnel should understand incident management and incident response and the difference between the two. Although closely related, incident response is a technical activity while incident management is a business function.

Attempting incident response with no sound incident management process will likely be overwhelmed by frequent requests from stakeholders for status updates. One won't work well if the other is not handled properly.

Incident response requires a documented process that should always be followed. The activity requires both drilling and testing. When an incident happens today, it might seem easy to remember the steps that should be done to contain it, but during a real breach, stress levels can rise substantially. That's why it's important to have a checklist that can be followed to ensure that tasks are done according to the intended order. To do that, document everything of importance during the incident. That way, there's something to refer to when another attack happens.

Another important factor in a better organization is to deploy a Security Information and Event Management system or SIEM. This can be used to collect, analyze, and automate logs. A SIEM might seem costly especially to small businesses but open-source SIEM systems are also available. One example would the SecurityOnion Linux distribution which already comes with OSSIM, a free-to-use SIEM product.

Educating the Staff

Training data center staff on how to act during an incident could not be emphasized enough. All incident responders and incident managers need to undergo regular training and drilling and these activities need to be done in the environments they manage.

An effective drill will be to do incident dry runs wherein incident responders and incident managers go through a simulated incident. These types of exercises can help the organization detect deficiencies in resource availability, procedures, and training.

With so many attack vectors, technologies, best practices, and cautions to consider, it's important for data center managers to keep end-users in the loop. Consider the scenario wherein user credentials have been stolen. Affected users should be told to change their passwords immediately. They should also be informed if there are applications that employ weak password controls and continued usage of those applications might put them at risk. There might even be scenarios that these applications should be totally locked down.

Some security experts agree that the best strategy to safeguard the data center perimeter is assuming that the perimeter itself doesn't exist and each component of the data center should be protected. Businesses should also deploy security measures that are server-specific with configured default-deny policies on each server within the data center. Security software and antivirus used on end-user computers won't be enough since, by default, they allow all items to pass through while blocking malicious items. Server security tools should instead block everything while only allowing approved items to execute.

In this context, the entire infrastructure should be hardened in such a way that virtual and physical servers will only be allowed to communicate using specific IP addresses, protocols, and ports. Also, an application whitelisting system should be deployed which blocks applications from running except when they're included in the list. Configuration and file integrity monitoring can also be used to detect suspicious administrative role actions or attempted changes as they happen in real-time.

Consider Everything

If a serious security breach happens, no stone should be left unturned during the investigation process. One strategy being used by attackers recently calls for burying malware deep inside the data center and letting it lay dormant for some time after it has been inserted. This way, when the attack is discovered and cleanup efforts have been carried out, it remains inside and unnoticed. Several financial institutions have fallen prey to this type of attack. Using the malware, the perpetrators were able to quietly withdraw money in small amounts over the course of a few months through different accounts. The withdrawals were small enough not to draw attention but it accumulated to millions after the attack is over.

Every piece of evidence related to the attack should be checked. This should be done until the attackers have been uncovered, compromised hosts have been identified, and the tools and tactics used have been understood. It might be time-consuming and tedious but using this approach, much can be learned about the incident which can be used to prepare for subsequent incidents.

Chapter 15. Implementing a Cybersecurity Framework

Information is a vital part of any business. As more organizations turn digital, cybersecurity is also becoming one of the standard components. If sensitive or valuable information such as proprietary data, customer transactions, or employee records are compromised, the effect on the business can be very devastating.

That's why it has become increasingly important to take steps in protecting information by implementing a sound cybersecurity framework. Cybersecurity might seem daunting especially for small and medium-sized businesses, either because of limited technical knowledge or costs, it's essential that everyone in an organization adopt practices to protect digital property, both personal and the customers'.

Identify

The Identify Function helps an organization increase it's understanding of the available resources and the underlying risks.

Identify People Who Have Access

Determine people who already have and those that should have access to the company's information and technology. Check whether or not a password, administrative privilege, or a key is required. In order to collect the required information, review the current list of accounts and the accompanying privileges that those accounts have.

Be aware of all people who have access to the business. Unauthorized or unknown persons should never be allowed physical access to business computers. This includes maintenance personnel and cleaning crews. Network or computer repair personnel should always be supervised when they are working on business systems. Encourage employees to question unrecognized persons entering the office premises. If an unauthorized person gets physical access to an unlocked computer, he or she can steal sensitive, personal, and confidential data stored on that machine.

Lock up mobile devices and laptops physically when not in use. Most operating systems have an automatic system lock when the device is not used for a certain period of time. Position the computer monitor or use a privacy screen so people that are walking by won't be able to see the information displayed on the screen.

Do Background Checks

All prospective employees should undergo a full background check which may include criminal records or even credit standing. This is especially important for positions that require handling business funds. This request can be made directly to the FBI or an FBI-approved channel.

Encourage the existing employees to do background checks on themselves. Identity theft has become increasingly common and many people only become aware of it after doing their own background check.

If applicants are applying for jobs that require specific degrees or specializations, call the school indicated in their resumes and verify the actual degree, graduation date, and grades or GPAs obtained. If references have been provided, call them as well and verify the dates the applicants worked for their previous companies. This helps ensure that the applicants are being honest.

Setup Individual Accounts

Each user should be given a separate account and this includes any contractor that may need access to your computer system. Require unique, strong passwords to be used for these accounts. The use of individual accounts can make it easier to pinpoint the culprit if data loss or manipulation occurs. Employees performing only typical work functions should not be given administrative privileges. This will ensure that attempts to install unauthorized software, be it intentional or not, is hindered. Guest accounts can be given to those who require only very minimal privileges such as Internet access only.

Implement Information Security Procedures and Policies

Procedures and policies can be used to determine acceptable expectations and practices in business operations, train employees on information security requirements, and can help in the investigation if a security incident occurs. These security procedures and policies should be readily available to employees through employee manuals or handbooks.

The breadth and scope of the policies involved are dependent on the business type as well as the accountability and degree of control required by the management. To ensure that these policies comply with local regulations and laws, have a lawyer that is familiar with cyber law review them before publishing.

These security procedures and policies for cybersecurity should clearly define whatever the company's expectations are as far as protecting systems and information are concerned. The content should list all the resources and information that are essential and describe how all employees are expected to use and protect them.

A document stating that the procedures and policies are understood and to be followed strictly should be signed by all employees. The employees should also be made aware of any penalties that are associated with violating these procedures and policies. The employee HR files should include this signed agreement.

As there may be changes in the technology or the organization itself over a period of time, these procedures and policies should be reviewed annually and updated accordingly. If there are changes, all employees must be made aware and they need to sign the new policy to acknowledge that they understand it.

Protect

The Protect Function helps contain or limit the impact of a potential cybersecurity event.

Limit Employee Access

If possible, no employee should be allowed access to the entire business system (personnel, financial, manufacturing, inventory, etc.). Employees should only be allowed access to information and systems required for them to do their jobs. Likewise, no single individual should be able to initiate a transaction and also approve it. This limitation should include senior managers and executives.

The most common source of cybersecurity incidents are insiders – employees or other people who work for the business. Because these people are already known and trusted to access important systems and information, their actions can significantly harm the business, be it deliberate or unintentional. Protecting against this type of cybersecurity incident is important since it can be hard to detect.

An employee leaving the business should be stripped of all access to the company's systems or information. This includes surrendering the company ID, deleting or disabling the username or account used in all systems, changing combination locks or group passwords the employee might know, and surrendering keys given to the employee.

Install Power Protectors

Surge protectors are designed to prevent electric dips and spikes to protect electronic systems. Uninterruptible Power Supplies or UPS allows people to work after a power outage for a limited amount of time to save their work or data. UPSs also often come with surge protection. You should determine the type and size of UPS your business requires.

Ensure that critical network devices and computers are connected to a UPS. For less sensitive devices, surge protectors should be enough. Surge protectors and UPSs should be tested regularly according to manufacturers' recommendations.

Patch Systems Regularly

A vulnerability in any software application such as firmware, operating systems, or even just a plugin can be a venue for a cyberattack. Ensure that only applications that are required for you to run the business are installed and that these applications are updated or patched regularly. Software vendors usually release regular updates and patches for their products which correct security issues or improve functionality. All software should be updated or patched regularly and this applies to all devices owned or used by the business.

Newly purchased computers should be immediately checked for the latest updates. The same goes for new software. Ensure that you are installing the latest and vendor-supported applications. Unsupported products will not receive updates from the vendors. A good example will be Windows XP which reached its end-of-support on April 8, 2014. Microsoft no longer provides patches for this operating system even though it has been found to have the Msoft WLFS vulnerability.

To have a regular patching schedule, assign a day in each month and check for updates. You can utilize tools that scan systems and report if there are available updates for applications installed. You can also check for new updates from the software manufacturers' websites.

Install Network Firewalls

Firewalls are used to block unwanted network traffic like browsing inappropriate sites or malicious communications, depending on how they are configured. You should install and configure a hardware-based firewall between the Internet and your internal network. Some wireless access points or routers may already have this functionality or it can be provided by your Internet Service Provider or ISP through their modem/router. There are also vendors who specialize in providing firewall routers, firewall wireless access points or routers, and firewall-only devices. You should also ensure that an antivirus application is installed with the firewall.

To further secure these devices, ensure that you change the administrator password right after installation and change it on a regular basis. You may also want to change the administrator's user name from the default. For attackers, knowing the user account is winning half the battle since they only have to guess the password to gain access to your firewall and eventually, the whole network.

As an additional security layer, you might also want to install and configure a software firewall on computers used in the business. This might also include smartphones and other devices that are connected to the network. If the option is available, enable logging of all traffic that goes through the firewall. The logs can be used if ever a post-attack investigation is required. Most operating systems have a built-in software firewall but these may need to be configured to enable logging.

Ensure that you always have the most current version of the software and hardware firewall systems and that they are authentic and supported by the vendor.

Even you use a virtual private network or VPN or hire the services of a cloud service provider, it's still necessary for each computer and network devices to have firewalls installed and configured. If you allow your employees to work at or from home, you should make sure that their home computer and network systems are protected by hardware and/or software firewalls and that these are configured appropriately and updated regularly.

Intrusion Detection / Prevention System or IDPS can also be installed in addition to a firewall. These are devices or systems specifically designed to analyze network traffic in more detail so they provide a more effective level of protection compared to firewalls.

Secure Networks and Wireless Access Points

To secure your wireless network, follow these tips to set up your wireless router.

- Immediately change the administrative password upon installation

- Configure the wireless access point so that its Service Set Identifier or SSID is not being broadcast.

- Do not use Wired-Equivalent Privacy as an encryption method. Instead, set the router to encrypt communications using WiFi Protected Access 2 or WPA-2 with Advanced Encryption Standard or AES.

To configure the settings listed above, check the user manual for the wireless router.

If you want to provide wireless Internet access to guests or customers, it should be in a separate network.

Avoid using unsecured or unknown wireless access points, even for non-business activities. Connect only to wireless access points that you trust or own.

If you have users connecting to unknown networks or working from home, implement an encrypted virtual private network or VPN to allow secure communication between their devices and the corporate network.

User Email and Web Filters

Email filters can be used to remove emails containing malware and other malicious content and also undesired or unsolicited ones, e.g. spam mails. Web filters work like email filters and notify the users if they are accessing websites that may contain malware or inappropriate content as per company policy.

Using web filters, you can block employees from visiting websites that are usual sources of cybersecurity threats such as social media or pornographic sites. By blocking access to these sites, you are preventing users from wasting business resources, conducting illicit activity, and downloading malware accidentally or intentionally. Most routers and firewalls can also be configured to block (blacklist) or allow (whitelist) certain addresses. You can download blacklists online or you can get it as part of the security service from your provider.

Encrypt Sensitive Business Data

Encrypting electronically stored data makes it unreadable to anyone without the use of an encryption key and/or password. Whenever possible, implement full-disk encryption on all computers, smartphones, and tablets. This encrypts all the data in the storage media. Most systems have built-in full-disk encrypting capabilities but not all mobile devices have it.

Remind the users to not forget or lose the encryption password or key. Losing the encryption key can mean losing data forever. Users should be instructed to save copies of their encryption keys or passwords and keep them in a secure location.

If you are sending sensitive or confidential emails or documents, consider end-to-end mail encryption. Most email and document applications already have this feature built-in. The receiver must use the same application that was used to encrypt the message in order to decrypt it. If the key or password needs to be provided in order to open the document or email, it should be provided through phone or other methods like secure messaging. It should not be sent included in the same email that contains the encrypted document.

Dispose of Old Media and Computers Safely

Your business might need to donate, throw away, or sell old computers and/or media. When disposing of old business systems, ensure that data is erased from all storage media using an electronic wipe. Most operating systems have this feature and there are third-party applications that can do this as well. If for some reason, you can't wipe the data from the hard drive, you can try degaussing it.

After data has been wiped from the hard drive, it should be removed from the computer and then physically destroyed. You can then recycle, donate, or sell the computer after the media has been removed. There are companies who will shred old media for you but you should be able to supervise the whole process.

The same applies to old removable media like USB drives, floppy disks, CDs, etc.). Sensitive personal or business data must first be removed before the media is physically destroyed under your supervision. For printed media, you can use a crosscut shredder or even consider incinerating them.

Implement a remote-wiping system on your mobile devices like laptop computers, smartphones, and tablets. If the device gets stolen or is lost, the system can wipe all data stored in the device so they can't be retrieved or extracted.

Train the Employees

As soon as employees are hired, they should undergo training on the existing information security procedures and policies and what is expected from them in order to protect the company's information and technology. They should sign an agreement stating that they understand the policies as well as the penalties involved when these are violated.

Here are things to include in the training:

- What they can and cannot do with company computers as well as mobile devices like accessing personal emails, visiting social media websites, etc.

- What is the expectation from them as far as treating business or customer information is concerned, for example if they can take data home or not.

- What they should do if a security or emergency incident occurs.

- Basic cybersecurity practices

The knowledge included in the training should be continuously reinforced during regular meetings or conversations. Monthly or quarterly meetings, training, newsletters, or seminars, on specific security-related subjects, can help reinforce this knowledge and embed a security 'culture' amongst employees.

Detect

The Detect Function contains activities that can help in the timely detection of cybersecurity events.

Install Anti-virus and Other Anti-malware Programs

Malware, which is short for malicious code or malicious software, is a computer code that is written with the intent to harm or steal. It includes spyware, viruses, and ransomware. There is malware that only consumes computer resources making systems slow but there are others that are designed to record actions on the computer and send sensitive and personal data to attackers.

Each device used in the business must have anti-malware installed and should be kept updated regularly. These devices include computers, mobile phones, and tablets.

If the option is available, set the anti-malware program to automatically check for available updates in real-time or at least on a daily basis. Full or complete scans should be automatically done after an update is installed and done on a daily basis preferably when the computer is idle so that it doesn't interfere with the users' daily tasks. Downloading updates may require that each computer is connected to the Internet using a fast connection or a server where the update is downloaded and then distributed to all computers in the network.

If employees are allowed to work at home using their personal devices, ensure that your corporate anti-malware programs are installed on those devices.

You can also implement two anti-malware solutions from different vendors to improve the chances of detecting viruses. Firewalls, routers, and Intrusion Detection/Prevention Systems may also have antivirus capabilities but you should not rely entirely on them for the protection of the whole network.

Maintain Logs

Protection and detection software and hardware usually keep logs of all activities in the monitored system. You should make sure that this logging feature is enabled. These logs might become useful when you need to verify suspicious activities or during post-attack investigations. Logs should be regularly backed up and the backup retained for at least a year.

Hiring the services of a cybersecurity professional to analyze the logs might help you detect unwanted or unusual trends like excessive visits to social media sites or a particular computer that is usually infected. Trends like these may indicate the need for increased protection in some areas of the network.

Respond

The Respond Function contains activities that can be done to reduce or contain the impact of a cybersecurity event.

Develop a Plan

Strategize a plan on what actions should be immediately taken in case of a medical emergency, fire, natural disaster, or burglary. This plan should include:

- Roles. Responsibilities should be clearly stated and the roles assigned to specific people in the business such as who contacts the police officers or who decides when recovery procedures should be initiated.

- What to do with information systems. This includes locking or shutting down computers, physically removing essential documents, moving to a relocation site, and others.

- Who to call. How and when to call emergency personnel, senior executives, legal professionals, cybersecurity professionals, insurance providers, service providers, etc. should be clearly defined in the plan. Ensure that contact information is included in the plan and that it is updated accordingly.

  There are states where 'notification laws' are enforced. If your business is in one of these states, you should let the customers know if there is any possibility that their information is lost, disclosed, or stolen. Ensure that this is stated in the plan as well.

  Notify the appropriate authorities if required. If it's possible that intellectual property, personal information, or other sensitive data is stolen, the local police department should be contacted for report filing.

- Indications of a security incident. List scenarios where a possible cybersecurity incident has occurred such as the company website being down for a certain period of time or if there's evidence that information has been stolen.

Recover

The Recover Function contains activities that can help an organization get back to normal operations after a security incident.

Make Full Backups

On a monthly basis at least, make full and encrypted data backups of each computer as well as mobile devices used in the business. This should be done immediately after a full virus scan to ensure that no infected files are getting backed up. Store the backups in a secure location away from the office so that whatever happens to the office such as theft, fire, or natural disasters, the data is safe and can be used to recover the system to its former state.

Backups can be used to restore in the incident of a malicious application infecting a system, an employee makes a mistake and deletes an important file or the computer breaks. If there are no backups, the only resort is manually recreating the business for paper records, if there are even any left. Data that should be backed up should include, but not limited to, system logs, accounts payable/receivable files, electronic spreadsheets, word processing documents, and other data that is generated by the business. Backup the data only. The applications can be reinstalled.

You can store backups on portable media, like USB drives, or via a cloud storage provider. If you opt for a cloud backup, you should encrypt your data first before storing in the cloud.

If you're using an external hard drive to back your data up, it should have enough capacity to hold the monthly backups for at least a year. Create separate folders for each of the computers being backed up. When connecting the external drive in a computer to back it up, copy the data into the correct designated folder.

You should test the backup data immediately after generating it in order to ensure that backup was complete and successful. This ensures that data can be restored if ever it's needed.

Make Incremental or Differential Backups of Important Data

Incremental or differential backup only logs the changes that have been made since the latest backup. These types of backup take less time than full backups so it can be done on a more frequent basis without interrupting normal operations. This means you can have a more recent backup than a monthly one. Conduct incremental or differential backups on business computer systems that hold critical data that is constantly updated like emails and financial data. Many advanced backup systems can do this on a regular basis for you.

Incremental and differential backups can be stored on:

- Removable media such as external hard drive, backup tape, etc.

- A separate machine or server that is not connected to the network

- Cloud storage provider via the Internet

Retain Data for 6 Months or More

Retaining data for 6 months or more allows you to restore data further back in time in case you need information that has been written over or deleted recently. This will require a storage device that can hold a lot of data. Let's say that you plan to retain at least a year of data, you should invest in storage that has at least 12 times the amount of data you currently have. Retaining backup longer also gives you more options in case a more recent backup gets corrupted.

Backups should be periodically tested for integrity. This ensures that you have reliable data in case you need to restore it after a security incident or a disaster.

Cyber Insurance

Cyber insurance can help the business respond to and even recover after a security incident. It's like any other type of insurance like fire or flood insurance that you may already have for the business. Some cyber insurance companies even offer cybersecurity services helping you identify areas of vulnerability, what actions should be taken to protect and secure your systems, and assist you during a security incident investigation.

You should do due-diligence if you are considering to purchase cyber insurance as you would other types of insurance. Determine the risks involved and also do research on the provider offering the protection, the services that they provide, the events that will be covered, and the provider's reputation on meeting contractual agreements.

Make Improvements

Cybersecurity should be a continuous process and improvements should be done as you learn about areas of possible security concerns. Assess the technology solutions, procedures, and processes regularly according to the risks. Make improvements and corrections as necessary.

Conduct training or exercises where you can simulate a major security incident scenario so you can identify possible weaknesses in personnel readiness, technology, procedures, and processes. You can then make adjustments as needed.

Chapter 16. Security and Safety at Work

Your company can prevent many incidents by practicing secure and safe business habits. In the previous chapter, we discussed the programmatic steps that can be taken within the business. This section discusses everyday activities that all employees should do to ensure that the business is secure and safe.

Cybercriminals are becoming more and more sophisticated but most of them still utilize well-known methods that are easily avoidable. Here are some recommended practices that you can implement to protect the business.

Pay Attention to People

Get to know and maintain contact with the employees and any contractors the building or business may employ for maintenance, security, cleaning, etc. Watch out for warning signs or unusual activities such a people becoming overly secretive, asking for too much overtime, working during unusual hours, or mentioning financial problems. In most instances, these actions may be benign, but there might be a case that indicates the employee is stealing money or information or damaging the business.

Be on the lookout for unusual activities in the industry or near the place of your business. Be aware of other companies conducting activities that may pose a safety or environmental risks. An incident that affects the area may affect the business or indicate risks. That's why it's important to be always vigilant.

Be Careful of Web Links and Email Attachments

One of the most effective ways for attackers to distribute malware is via web links or attachments in emails that's why it's pretty common. Often, the attackers attach the malware to an email and make it look like it's coming from someone or something the receiver knows. This is known as phishing. Weblinks can also be altered to make them look like legitimate ones allowing download of the malware from a malicious site controlled by attackers.

Do not open an attachment or click on a link on an email that you're not expecting. If it appears to be legitimate or important, contact the sender via other means to verify the email that you received and have the sender describe to you what the link or attachment is and what is it for.

Before clicking a link that you see on websites, instant messages, or social media, hover the mouse cursor over the link. The actual website address or URL where you will be taken to will be displayed at the bottom of your browser. If you don't trust the address or don't recognize it, try to search for relevant keywords instead. You will find the info you're looking for that way without clicking on a suspected link. Train the employees in recognizing phishing methods and notifying the right person if there is suspicion of such an activity.

Use Separate Accounts

If possible, use business devices and accounts for business activities and use personal devices and accounts for personal activities. This is important especially if other people have access to your personal devices such as your partner or your children. Don't conduct sensitive or business activities such as online business banking on personal devices. Likewise, don't engage in personal activities such as downloading videos, gaming, web surfing, or social media on business devices. Sending sensitive business data to personal email addresses should also be prohibited.

Personal devices are typically less secure than business systems. This is because they may be used to visit untrustworthy websites and be installed with untrusted applications and games which are not necessary for work and can be exploited by hackers due to vulnerabilities.

Most cyberattacks require connection to the network which means they can be prevented by disconnecting a system from the network. That's why some businesses build computers that are isolated from other machines in the network which can be used for handling sensitive business information.

Do Not Use Personal Storage Devices

Like personal computers and mobile devices, sharing external hard drives and USB drives between business and personal devices should be prohibited. Do not connect untrusted or unknown hardware into either personal or business systems. This applies to removable media as well. Attackers may place USB drives in places where they can be found by potential victims. These may be labeled in such a way as to stir interest luring the founder into inserting it in a computer to see what it contains. What the malicious USB device may then do is log keyboard and mouse activities in that computer or install malware to take control of the machine.

The Autorun feature allows applications to be automatically launched when a USB device or installation media is inserted. This can be a venue for malware so it should be disabled.

Check What You Download

If you don't trust the website, don't download anything from it. Ensure that all employees only download from reputable business websites as these can be considered safe. Be careful with downloading shareware or freeware. Some of these can be compromised and contain adware that will be installed together with the application. These may also open up more vulnerabilities in the system.

Don't Give Out Business and Personal Info

Another method used by attackers is called social engineering. The plan is to obtain electronic or personal access to business data through people manipulation. A common type of this attack is an email, website, or a person pretending to be someone or something. A social engineer will do extensive research about the business to know more about names, responsibilities, titles, and other personal information that can be gathered using this method. Using the acquired information, the social engineer then stages an attack by sending an email or calling with a believable story, although made-up, in order to lure the victim to give out certain information.

If you get a phone call wherein you're being asked for personal information and that the caller says he or she is from a company that you recognize, such as your doctor's office or the bank, ask for the caller's name and the division they're in. Then call the number indicated on that company's website and look for the person to confirm his or her identity.

Train the employees to never respond to unsolicited phone calls asking for business or personal information. They should also notify the management if ever such an attempt was made.

No company should be asking for username and password for any reason. Attackers may also ask what operating system you have, or the firewall brand you use, or even what applications is installed in your systems. They can then use this information to exploit vulnerabilities to break into your network or system.

Watch for Malicious Pop-ups

Pop-up windows might appear as you browse the Internet asking you to click on a button. Enable the popup blocker in the web browser you're using and allow pop-ups only from trusted websites.

If a pop-up window appears unexpectedly, do not click on any part of it including the X in the upper right corner. These windows might state that you've won a prize, a virus has been found on your machine, or you need to download a driver or codec to continue to the website. These pages are designed to accept any click on its window as your agreement to download and install an application which is most probably malware.

To close this window, disconnect from the network and close the application from the Task Manager. This is done by pressing ctrl+alt+del simultaneously if you're using Microsoft Windows, and launching the Task Manager. You can then close the application forcefully. You should then save open files and reboot the machine. Immediately run a full virus scan after the computer starts up.

User Strong Passwords

Stronger passwords mean it will be harder for attackers to hack it using a brute-force or dictionary attack. A good password contains a random sequence of uppercase and lowercase letters, numbers, and characters. It should also be at least 12 characters long.

For systems that host sensitive information, implement multi-factor authentication or MFA. When MFA is used, an additional layer of authentication is required during authentication. For example, after a user logs in with a username and password, a text message will be sent containing a code that needs to be entered to complete the authentication process. You may also implement biometrics authentication (e.g. fingerprint scanners).

Most devices come with a preset administration password. You should change this immediately after installation and configuration, and also regularly thereafter. Using the default administration password will make it easier for attackers to gain access to your systems and take control of them. Consult the manual on how to change the default administration password.

Periodic and mandatory password changed should be implemented. The longer the password is left unchanged, the more time hackers have to crack it. Or the password may be shared with co-employees. Implement a periodic password change every 3 months at the least. You can enforce this on some systems so that users are required to change their passwords according to the schedule you configured.

Password reuse also makes it easy for hackers to get into multiple systems. Train employees not to use the same password when accessing systems that host sensitive business information. If a hacker is able to get into a machine using a password and it's the same one configured on multiple systems, the attacker gets access to those as well. It can get difficult to remember different passwords for different accounts so you might consider purchasing a password management system. Be aware, though, that this system becomes a central repository of accounts and passwords being used to access systems that host sensitive data so these credentials may get compromised or get lost.

Secure Online Transactions

Online banking, commerce, or business should be done via secure browser connections. A website is secure when you can see a small lock in the upper left or lower right corner of the browser.

Get into the habit of deleting your web browser history, cookies, temporary Internet files, and cache regularly. This is more important if you used a public computer or when you just finished an online banking or commerce activity. By doing this, important and sensitive information won't get stolen if the system gets compromised. Deleting these files also make your computer run faster. You can do the cleanup through the browser's security or privacy menu. You can consult the help section of your browser on how this is done.

If you process a lot of online business banking transactions, consider assigning a dedicated system that will only be used for similar activities. This computer might not be used for personal activities like accessing email, doing personal banking, or Internet searches. Use it solely for online banking and disconnect it from the network when not in use to minimize the possibility of an attack.

Chapter 17. Understanding and Managing Risks

Risks are a collection of vulnerabilities, threats, the probability of a security incident, and how such an incident will affect the business. We all make decisions every day that are considered risk-based. When we drive to work, for example, we assess vulnerabilities and threats such as traffic and weather conditions, the reliability and safety features of our car, and the skill of drivers.

If you understand the risks involved, it's easier to determine where to put more focus. Although completely eliminating security risks might be difficult or even impossible, the goal of your cybersecurity program is to make informed decisions in relation to information security by assessing the risks involved and implementing measures to minimize them.

Understanding your risks completely and perfectly is impossible. There will be scenarios when you will need to exert a huge effort as you try to assess the risks. That's why it's important that you utilize every resource available to you. This includes information sharing organizations, knowledge experts, and relevant stakeholders.

Risk Elements

In cybersecurity, threats are things that can negatively affect the information required to run the business. Threats can occur in the form of natural or personnel events which means they can accidental or intentional. Here are some of the most common cybersecurity threats:

- Environmental – earthquake, tornado, water, fire

- Business resources – employees, supply chain disruption, equipment failure

- Hostile actors – hackers, hacktivists, nation-state actors, criminals

If you look at the types of threats listed above, it may not be easy to understand how they can be related to cybersecurity. For example, consider what happens in the event of a flood. Paper documents, servers, and computers can be destroyed by even just a little amount of water. In the case of a large flood, you may not be able to collect or protect the information required for your business to run.

Vulnerabilities are weaknesses that can be exploited in order to harm the business. Any scenario wherein data is not sufficiently protected relates to vulnerability. Most cybersecurity breaches are made possible because of vulnerabilities. We've already discussed how to minimize vulnerabilities and reduce the impact of a cybersecurity incident in a previous couple of chapters.

There are threats that affect industries and businesses differently. A retailer who does most of the organization's business online will be more threatened by website defacement compared to an organization with little to no web presence.

Likelihood is the probability a threat will affect the organization and helps you to come up with which protections you should put in place.

Also, the type of information being processed by businesses differs may differ from one organization to the other. If a digital copy of a marketing brochure, for example, has been leaked to the Internet, it may not harm the business as much as leaked proprietary business information or sensitive customer data. The impact a security incident can have on the company depends on the industry, the business, and the information affected.

Managing the Risks

Risk management is the act of identifying the type of information at hand and the level of protection required, and implementing that protection and monitoring the progress. We'll be discussing simple steps on how you can manage security risks by coming up with an information security program based on the risks involved.

Risk management will need the inclusion of personnel from different areas of the business and the collaboration between them for this program to be successful. People that you should consider bringing in the fold are those that have the capability to make informed decisions like IT personnel, legal counselors, corporate executives, and project managers. You may also include your customers, especially those you do a lot of business interactions with so you can tap them as additional resources.

You should have an annual review and update of the risk management plan and when there are plans to implement changes that may affect the whole program such as purchasing new IT systems, procedural changes, or starting a new project. Also, when a security incident happens to one of the business' employees, customers, suppliers (especially those you buy software or computer equipment from), or business partners, assess the scenario to ensure that you still have adequate protection in place.

Identifying the type of information that the business uses and stores

It's unreasonable and even impossible to implement protection on all the pieces of information that flows through and inside the business against all the threats out there. That's why should only focus on which information you consider is the most valuable for the business. This step is the most important and also usually the most challenging part of risk management.

You can begin by listing down all the types of information that are processed by your business. 'Information type' can be defined in any way that is useful or makes sense to the organization. For example, you may have the employees make a list of all the information they work on regularly. List anything that comes into your mind but they don't have to be too specific. Examples would customer names and their email addresses, the business' banking information, raw materials receipts, and other proprietary information

Determining the value of the information

Now that you have identified the different information types that the business needs to function, assess these instances and the effect on the organization.

- What if the information has been made public?

- What if the information was incorrect?

- What if the information couldn't be accessed by the customers?

These questions are related to the information type's confidentiality, integrity, and availability and will help you assess a security incident's potential impact.

Chapter 18. Responding to a Cybersecurity Incident

Every single business in today's environment is reliant on telecommunications and technology, to some extent. Because of this, all companies are susceptible to cyberattacks. Sooner or later your business will go through a cybersecurity incident. It's not a matter of 'if' but a matter of when.

Nowadays, cybersecurity is a concern for all industries and businesses that it has become a board-level item in meeting agendas. Cyberattacks affect the business as a whole. It's not just a technical issue but also an operational and a people issue.

In 2015, at least a million web attacks were recorded on a daily basis and more than 75% of websites have been found with vulnerabilities. Cybercrimes are getting more common as attackers become more innovative. Cyberattacks are here to stay and hackers are not slowing down. Problem is, a lot of companies are still not prepared or equipped to fend off cyberattacks.

Quick and comprehensive action is essential to containing a cybersecurity incident. Doing so ensures that the company is not exposed to greater liability. Cybersecurity professionals are the business' first and last line of defense.

During an attack on eBay, hackers were able to steal personal information of more than 233 million users. It could have ended it all for the company. To minimize the damage, eBay assured the users that their financial information is separately encrypted and was safe. They also encouraged users to immediately change their passwords in order to prevent more attacks.

When a cyberattack happens, you must take critical steps to deal with the incident.

Planning for the Worst

When a cyberattack happens, you should ensure that the fallout is minimal. To do this, all employees must know what role they should play in managing this crisis.

This is why you need to come up with a crisis management plan designed for cyberattacks which you can deploy as soon as a cyberattack happens. The plan should include securing the network, limiting the damage, and starting the recovery process in case of data or system loss.

As new technologies and tools emerge, this crisis handling plan should be continually upgraded and people in the business should be made aware of these changes.

Mobilizing Your Response Team

A response team to handle the cybersecurity incident should be formed. This team should include people coming from relevant stakeholder groups – IT, communications, and operations departments. Each of the team members will have clearly defined roles as well as an action plan that will be carried out immediately after the attack.

To form the team, for example, technical personnel will be tasked to investigate the breach, employee and HR representatives will handle employee-affecting breaches, intellectual property will help recover stolen product information or minimize the impact on brand, and data protection experts will manage personal data. External representatives may also need to be involved if the internal teams don't have sufficient capacity or capability.

Representatives from the company's legal team or even external counsel should also be included in the incident response team. A cyberattack may come with some legal implications so it's important for the business to ask legal advice immediately after a cyberattack has been discovered.

Existing insurance policies purchased by the business will need to be checked to confirm if losses due to a cyberattack are covered. If insurance is in place, the policies need to be reviewed whether the insurance company should be notified immediately about the breach. Some insurance policies will cover remedial and legal costs only on the notification date.

Identifying the Attack

To understand the source, breadth, and impact of the breach, the type of cyberattack should first be determined. This will give you an idea of how to formulate your action plan.

For example, if an attacker was able to obtain information from one of the employees using social engineering methods, the employee concerned should be consulted to determine what information was given to the attacker. In a scenario wherein a disgruntled employee is the identified attacker, identify all accounts assigned to that person and determine access levels associated with those accounts to assess potential damage.

Securing the Systems

Once the breach has been identified, the next step will be securing the IT systems. This will help contain the attack and ensure that it's not progressing.

There are scenarios wherein you need to suspend or isolate a section of your network temporarily to contain the damage. In worst cases, you may even need to shut the whole network down. Although this can be costly for the company and disruptive to its normal operations, it's necessary.

It's also important to determine when the breach happened and how wide it has affected the whole network and systems infrastructure. There should be tools in place in the organization that detects intrusions as soon as they happen.

Investigating the Attack

Investigating the attack will include gathering information surrounding the breach, the effects of the incident to the whole organization, and which remedial actions have been taken. The management will decide on who should lead the investigation and ensure that appropriate resources are provided to the investigating body.

If an employee has been found to be involved in the breach, the investigation process will also need to consider applicable labor laws. This means consulting and involving representatives from the HR department as needed.

The investigating team should ensure that all activities are documented. If any regulatory notification needs to be submitted, these documents may be required. Investigations are often repetitive. As the surrounding circumstances become clearer, further inquiry becomes more apparent.

Whenever a breach occurs, the results of the investigation should be used to modify the existing procedures and policies as well as the incident response plan. The employees should then be notified about the changes and training should be initiated.

Managing Public Relations

If your business is consumer-facing, managing public relations will be a key role of the response team. Although not all breaches will be made known to the public, most of them will be inevitable. These include your customers' personal data being compromised and published in public domain, or pertinent data protection laws requiring you to notify the individuals affected by the breach.

To minimize further damage, it's important to be timely and accurate in managing public announcements. The management should also be honest and open regarding the incident.

You should issue a press release and discuss the details of the breach and how you were able to resolve it. Doing this helps direct the narrative and it's a way of getting ahead of the story. This also shows transparency to avoid accusations of attempted cover-ups or secrecy.

Addressing Regulatory and Legal Requirements

Some laws concerning cybersecurity might require regulatory notification in case a breach happens. As of yet, most jurisdictions, may not have all-encompassing or specific cybersecurity laws. But the increased frequency and accelerated evolution of threats have given birth to a patchwork of regulations and laws.

Some of the laws apply across all sectors but there are also legislations that are industry-specific that have been put in place in relation to sectors that are most at risk. These businesses include telecommunications, critical utility infrastructure, and financial services.

In the United States, the Cybersecurity Framework was developed by the National Institute of Standards and Technology. This consists of practices, guidelines, and standards that promote the management and protection of vital system infrastructures. Another legislation, Executive Order 13636, expands the current program for collaboration and information sharing between the private sector and the government.

In Europe, businesses should pay attention to data protection laws. The Data Protection Regulation, for example, entails an obligation for businesses across all sectors to inform the concerned data protection authority about the security breach. The report should include details regarding the breach, its effects on the business, and the remedial actions that have been taken.

There is also brewing legislation in Europe which is an upgrade to the Cyber Security Directive, which will require market operators (e.g. banking/financial, transport, gas, oil, electricity, etc.) to report cybersecurity incidents to appropriate authorities.

Some laws may require, aside from the regulatory notification, that the individuals who own the compromised data also be notified in case of a breach. The problem is, the decision on who should be notified is not that easy. It might even be impossible to confirm the owner of the affected data. If the business has millions of customers, notifying all of them is not something to be taken lightly as it would have a devastating impact on the integrity of the company.

Incurring Liability

No matter how much your business has prepared for it, you will incur liability in some form after a security incident and there are different ways that it could happen.

A direct, non-legal liability can be a consequence of a cybersecurity incident. This type of liability arises, through theft, blackmail attempts, ex-gratia payments, and ransomware that the business may choose to pay from a customer relationship and public relations perspective. Ransomware and ex-gratia payments may be a major cost to businesses after a cyberattack but it might be necessary in order to mitigate damage to customer relationships. For example, the business may offer free, limited-time credit screening for customers whose credit card details were compromised after a breach.

With new laws governing cybersecurity being put into place, breaches will often have a corresponding regulatory liability. In the EU, for example, there are laws requiring businesses to implement appropriate organizational and technical security measures dedicated to protecting personal data. If this regulatory requirement has not been implemented, there's a corresponding a hefty fine. According to the Data Protection Act 1998 in UK, £500,000 is the maximum fine. During Sony's PlayStation breach in 2011, the UK Information Commissioner imposed a £250,000 fine.

However, if the upgraded Data Protection Regulation currently being proposed becomes effective, the maximum fine can be 5% of the business' annual global turnover or €100 million, whichever is greater.

There are also regulations that are sector-specific. In the financial service sector in the UK, for example, higher fines have been imposed by regulators compared to the Information Commissioner. In August 2010, Zurich Insurance Plc was fined £2.275 million after the company lost almost 50,000 customer records stored in a backup tape with no encryption in place. This happened when the tape was on its way to a South African branch.

Cybersecurity breach liabilities can be incurred during litigation of negligence and breach of equitable duties, contract, or statutory obligations. Most of the cases related to this type of liability happened in the US. For example, the court required Target to pay $10 million as a settlement for a class-action lawsuit during the 2013 breach.

Repairing Customer Relationships

Even after the cyberattack has been detected and the vulnerabilities patches, your customers may not be likely to trust you immediately. This is where transparency comes in.

Keep the customers updated with all the ongoing news and communications about what has been and is being done to patch the vulnerabilities. Inform them of the efforts to increase and improve security measures which will put their minds at ease.

Chapter 19. Case Study: Stuxnet

It was a very sophisticated computer worm designed to exploit multiple zero-day vulnerabilities in Microsoft Windows to infect computers and propagate. But it didn't stop at just infecting PCs. Stuxnet was programmed to cause physical effects in the real world. It specifically targeted centrifuges that are used to produce enriched uranium which powers nuclear reactors and weapons.

The information security community first recognized Stuxnet in 2010, although it's believed to have been developed as early as 2005. Although recognized for its impressive ability to spread and the widespread infection it caused, this worm does very little to no harm to systems that are not used in uranium enrichment.

When Stuxnet infects a computer, the worm checks if that system is connected to specific programmable logic controllers or PLCs that are manufactured by Siemens. Computers interact with PLCs in order to control industrial machinery such as uranium centrifuges. Stuxnet will then alter the programming of the PLC in such a way that the centrifuges are spun too fast and too long, which destroys or damages the equipment. All the while, the PLC tells the computer that the centrifuge is operating normally so it's difficult to diagnose or detect that's there something wrong.

The Stuxnet Creator/s

It's widely accepted in the cybersecurity community that Stuxnet was created through the combined efforts of the United States and Israel's intelligence agencies. This classified project meant to create the worm was code-named 'Operation Olympic Games'. The project was started during the term of President George W. Bush and then continued until the term of President

Obama. Neither the US nor Israel have ever officially admitted creating Stuxnet. However, Gabi Ashkenazi, head of the Israeli Defense Forces mentioned Stuxnet as one of the successes of his watch during the celebration of his retirement in 2011.

The software engineers behind Stuxnet's creation haven't been identified yet but they are apparently very skilled, and that it was a large group. Roel Schouwenberg of Kaspersky's Lab believes it took 2 to 3 years to develop and that there were at least ten programmers involved in the process.

After Stuxnet, other worms with the same infection capabilities were identified in the wild. A couple of them were called Flame and Duqu. The purposes of these worms may be different from that of Stuxnet's but the similarity in the behavior is a clue that the same developers designed these as well and they are still active.

Stuxnet's Purpose

Iran was in a rush to develop its own nuclear weapons and the Israel and US governments needed a tool to derail this activity or at least delay it. The administrations of Bush and Obama had the assumption that if Iran develops its own nuclear weapons, Israel will retaliate by launching airstrikes on Iranian nuclear facilities and this move will start a regional war. They needed a nonviolent alternative, thus, Operation Olympic Games were born. There were doubts that a worm can be created to affect physical infrastructure but during a dramatic meeting held with Bush during the later years of his presidency, pieces coming from a damaged test uranium centrifuge were presented. This evidence convinced the US government to give the green light on unleashing the malware.

The primary target of Stuxnet was the Natanz nuclear facility in Iran and it was never the intention to have it spread beyond the area. The area had no Internet connection and was air-gapped. For the computers inside to be infected, a USB stick containing the worm should be transported inside through intelligence agents or unwilling victims. This meant that it should have been very easy to contain.

For some reason, the worm did spread through the Internet and spread throughout the world because of its aggressive nature. As mentioned, damage to computers not connected to nuclear centrifuges is very minimal. How did it end up in the wild? Many speculate that the Israelis modified the code. This made then-Vice President Biden very upset according to reports.

The Source Code

Liam O'Murchu, Symantec's Security Technology, and Response group director were there when Stuxnet was first unraveled. According to his words, Stuxnet was "by far the most complex piece of code that we've looked at — in a completely different league from anything we'd ever seen before."

If you do a quick search, you'll see a lot of websites claiming to have the full Stuxnet code that you can download. O'Murchu said these are fakes or just a very small fragment of the sophisticated code. He also said that the real source code hasn't been leaked or released officially and that it's impossible to extract from the compiled binaries that are found in the wild.

Chapter 20. Case Study: 911 Service Crash

In March of 2018, the dispatch system of Baltimore's 911 service was attacked by a still unknown hacker or group of hackers. This led to a temporary halt on the automated dispatching which also prompted an investigation on how the breach happened according to the city's Mayor Catherine Pugh.

Pugh's spokesman, James Bentley, confirmed that the attack affected the messaging functions of the computer-controlled dispatch called the CAD system. No further comments were received from the mayor about the breach.

FBI spokesman Dave Fitz said the agency was notified about the breach and that they provided technical assistance.

According to city personnel, it was identified as a limited breach of the system. CAD supports Baltimore's 911 as well as 311 services. The attack happened on a weekend morning according to the Mayor's Office of Information Technology's chief information officer Frank Johnson. During the breach, the 911 and 311 services were put to manual mode so they were able to continue to operate without further disruption.

'This effectively means that instead of details of incoming callers seeking emergency support being relayed to dispatchers electronically, they were relayed by call center support staff manually," according to Johnson.

Johnson also said city personnel isolated the affected server and took it offline immediately which helped mitigate the threat. After a thorough investigation on the machine, they were able to fully restore the CAD system by 2 AM the following Monday.

As soon as the attack was noticed, Darryl De Sousa, Baltimore Police Commissioner was notified. Police commanders then deliberately turned off the majority of their online systems to avoid being compromised further. De Sousa also said the attack didn't lead to any slowdown as far as police response to incidents is concerned.

The following Tuesday, there was no response from the mayor's office as to what information might be compromised, if any. No information on other similar attacks, the hack's specific nature, or if there are already suspects were provided. They said the investigation was ongoing and providing more details might compromise the process.

The Baltimore 911 attack is just one of the many hacking incidents that have been plaguing systems across the US. A cyberattack on Atlanta City paralyzed their online bill payment system via a ransomware attack wherein hackers demanded a payment amounting to $51,000 in bitcoin currency before they release the system. A month before the incident, President Trump said the Russian government is behind these concerted hacking efforts which affected US utility systems as well as the country's power grid.

In Baltimore, they are using the CAD system to populate 911 callers' locations automatically using a mapping system. This makes connecting the callers to the nearest emergency responders faster and more efficient. This helps callers who are using their mobile phones and don't have any idea where they are exactly.

Systems like CAD also send out information usually received by dispatchers directly to the first responders themselves in some situations. These also log information for records and data retention.

When the CAD system is down, which is what happened in Baltimore during the attack, dispatchers will have to take the callers' information manually and they have nothing to compare it to ensure the accuracy. This makes the whole process much less efficient.

Although systems like CAD don't store much financial or personal data which are mostly targeted by hackers, these may contain medical information and can also provide back-door entry to mapping systems that are used by cities such as Baltimore. CAD systems are also critical to their ability to promptly respond in case of disasters.

NENA CEO Brian Fontes spoke about the importance of protecting systems like CAD. NENA is an association composed of 911 professionals in the US.

According to Fontes, an increase in attacks has been noted on 911 centers across the country and operators are now realizing the systems' vulnerabilities and coming to terms with them.

In 2015, the US Department of Homeland Security warned that the move of public safety answering points, or PSAPs, such as 911 to internet-based systems make them more vulnerable to cyberattacks.

There have been news reports on government website hacks and these have been increasing over the years. Several hacktivists have also been targeting local governments and cities for political reasons.

While PSAPs might not store valued information such as Social Security or credit card numbers, they usually store house addresses and names and sometimes even medical records. These can then be combined by hackers to get more damaging information.

There were even attacks on some 911 systems where attackers used mobile devices that have been compromised to send massive calls to 911 centers which overwhelms the system and makes it unavailable for legitimate calls. Other hackers take control of the system demanding ransom which is a similar case with the payment system of Atlanta City.

As of this writing, there are no further details on the Baltimore 911 system hack.

According to Fontes, their association stresses the importance of resiliency and redundancy on 911 systems. Many centers have begun migrating to improved technologies which will allow them full, normal operations using back-up systems in case of an attack.

Chapter 21. Case Study: ATM Attacks

Day after day, people working in information security have to confront with security alerts, more so for those employed in banking or other financial institutions. It's a fact that hundreds of thousands of attacks are faced by large banks every single day and it's never easy to choose which attacks security people can leave alone and which they should act on.

In August 2018, a confidential alert was sent by the FBI containing a warning that incoming ATM attacks are likely to hit banks very soon.

According to the FBI alert, they have obtained unspecified reports that indicate hackers are brewing up a global plan to attack automated teller machines or ATMs in the coming weeks. The attack is associated with a previous breach on an unknown card issuer which allows attackers 'unlimited operations'.

Unlimited attacks mean cybercriminals will phish or hack their way into bank systems or payment card processors according to Brian Krebs, a security blogger who made the FBI warning public.

Krebs said that before executing ATM cashouts, the attackers will disable fraud detection controls implemented by the financial institution which include the daily limit on transaction times as well as the maximum amount that can be withdrawn per day. The perpetrators will also try to alter security measures and customer account balances so they will be allowed to quickly remove cash in large amounts from the ATMs.

In the survey conducted by ATMIA from 2015 to 2017, ATM attacks have grown to as much as around 55%.

During an interview, Krebs also stated that in recent ATM attacks, the perpetrators were able to steal between 9 to 13 million dollars in just a few hours. He also speculated that according to the FBI warning, hackers will go through the compromised large payment processor to infiltrate small banks. Payment processors Visa and First Data, however, refused to comment on Krebs' statement.

Krebs said the criminal group plotting the concerted attacks on ATMs may have to coordinate with people on the ground to do the withdrawals and this may have alerted the FBI, thus the warning to the banks. Krebs also said that there's usually a flurry of activities right before the cashouts happen. Criminal types may get pinged by the attackers offering hundreds of dollars for a few hours of work which involved withdrawing from ATMs.

Bank of America, JPMorgan Chase, and Wells Fargo – who own the largest networks of ATM in the US – did not respond or refused to comment. No comments were also received from Diebold and NCR – two of the largest ATM manufacturers in the country.

ATM Industry Association's CEO, Mike Lee, said his team is already looking into this alert from the FBI. He stated that his team is uncertain as to whether or not the FBI warning was issued based on facts that have been verified. However, while they are conducting internal investigations in order to assess the degree of threat and the likelihood of the event recurring (or occurring in the first place), they urge ATM operators and networks to implement additional precautions and best practices in maintaining security.

A survey made by the organization in 2018 showed that at least 91% of the current ATMs have been improved to adapt to high-security systems as required by EMV standards and that most of those can already do chip-on-chip transactions.

According to the ATMIA's executive director for the Americas and US, David Tente, these new technologies will allow improved protection against counterfeit cards use on ATMs.

According to the FBI's warning, smaller banks will be most affected by the incoming attacks. Compromised in the past have involved small to medium-sized banks and financial institutions. This is most likely due to cybersecurity controls that are less robust than those in bigger banks, budget cuts, and vulnerabilities found in third-party systems. The FBI also expects that the frequency of these attacks will only increase in the future.

In a phishing attack made on the National Bankshares located in Blacksburg, Va., perpetrators were able to make off with at least $2.4 million out of the organization's $1.3 billion assets.

There have also been observations on attack trends on smaller banks which further proves that the FBI's warning should not be taken for granted.

When a small financial processor or institution is attacker, the hacker tries to compromise the debit card information on current or checking accounts, searches for the ATM PIN, records it on a new card or sells the data to another cybercriminal. The withdrawal controls or limits are then subverted and the attacker then gets the cash from the ATMs fast. It's very efficient and effective.

These hackers also tend to focus on old ATMs and retail ATMs that are unattended as shown by incidents of ATM hacking in the early months of 2018.

When an ATM has run out of cash, the bank gets an alert from the system. But this may not be the case with ATMs that are managed by third parties. Bank ATMs are more secure than nonbank ATMs, but the former also gets attacked.

Phishing is regarded as the most often starting point when it comes to ATM cash-out schemes. Attacks on ATMs and the whole banking infrastructure is in constant evolution with cybercriminals developing more sophisticated ways to orchestrate the attacks. But it usually starts with the same target – a person that gets victimized by credential phishing and other types of social engineering schemes. That's why financial institutions should prioritize the education of employees in spotting attacks through the web, social media, and email that are socially engineered. They should run phishing simulations that employ real-world tactics through fake attacks. This will help the organization to understand who amongst the employees are most likely to be victimized by this type of attack.

For attackers to be able to withdraw the money from ATMs, compromising the accounts should be in synch with the manufacturing of the fraudulent debit cards. When consumers use a smartphone app to access cash instead of a physical card, the access token becomes dynamic and changes each time a withdrawal request is made which makes the process more secure. Cardless cash transactions also usually require more secure authentication systems like biometric scanners.

Transactions through mobile phones can also be locked using geographic validation limiting the areas on which processes can be limited to specific countries. Mobile cash transfer or payment release can also be validated by another security later via phone call or text messages from the bank's system. Cards can also be locked using mobile phone apps to prevent usage until the account holder unlocks it.

Hacking mobile cardless transactions requires spoofing, not just the customer account but also the unique tokens exchanged between the mobile device and the system making it more difficult than manufacturing fake cards.

The FBI recommended the following activities to improve ATM security:

- Required strong passwords and implement multi-factor authentication using digital or physical tokens whenever possible for business-critical roles and system administrators.

- Establish role separations and implement multi-authentication procedures for balance inquiries and increases in withdrawals within a particular threshold.

- Limit unapproved applications installed in the infrastructure to minimize the propagation of malware.

- Limit, audit, and audit business-critical and administrator accounts.

- Monitor the use of administrative tools and remote network protocols used to connect to the network in conducting post-attack such as TeamViewer, Cobalt Strike, and Powershell.

- Check for encrypted data being transferred through nonstandard network ports.

- Monitor data traffic to regions where connections from financial organizations don't usually occur.

Chapter 22. Case Study: Flight Cancellations Due to Attacks

In June 2015, a cyberattack was done on Warsaw's Chopin Airport which caused flights to be canceled or delayed. During a weekend, LOT, a Polish airline, was forced to cancel and ground flights because their computer systems were targeted by a cyberattack. Repairing the damage took around five hours which affected a large number of passengers.

Although details of the attack were not published, Adrian Kubicki, a spokesman of LOT, said that the attackers temporarily paralyzed the airline's computer systems located at the airport, which delayed the processing of flights for passengers. Around 1400 passengers were affected by the said attack with flight schedules to Copenhagen, Dusseldorf, and Hamburg through at least a dozen delays and 10 flight cancellations.

To pacify the passengers' complaints, LOT transferred some of them to other flights and also provided hotels for those who stayed overnight. According to the airline spokesman, there were no compromised ongoing flights at other airports were not affected by the attack. Although LOT was already using cutting-edge computer systems, attackers were still able to breach into their security and this signals a threat to the airline industry.

Aviation cyberthreats are treated as critical because they might lead to loss of lives aside from the financial and operational effects. That's why these types of attacks should be taken seriously. This was the case with a passenger named Chris Roberts. He was banned by United Airlines to fly from Colorado to San Francisco after he tweeted that he can get into the onboard systems used by the airline. Chris said connections to the airline's system which can make viewing data containing flight management systems, fuel, and engines. United Airlines, however, insisted that their control systems were very secure and that unauthorized access is impossible.

In December 2014, the International Coordinating Council of Aerospace Industry Associations (ICCAIA), the International Air Transport Association (IATA), the Civil Air Navigation Services Organisation (CANSO), the Airports Council International (ACI), and the International Civil Aviation Organization (ICAO) all agreed to come up with a roadmap to counteract cyber threats. Through a cybersecurity agreement, they unanimously promoted a more robust cybersecurity strategy and culture which includes cybersecurity best practices, risk assessments, and threat identification.

Organizations have changed in the way cyberattack reports are being handled. In the case of LOT, they readily admitted that the 20 flight delays and cancellations were caused by a cyberattack. This used to be uncommon in the airline industry.

This raises concerns about what really happened at United Airlines in the same year. On June 2, 2015, all flights of United Airlines were grounded for at least an hour. Initially, the airline reported the case as caused by "faulty flight information in the airline's dispatch system," which they blamed on "automation issues." Some speculations published on Twitter stated that the grounding was caused by hacks that issued random and false flight plans. On July 8, United Airlines had to ground thousands of flights due to a network connectivity issue that lasted for nearly a couple of hours.

On July 29 of the same year, Bloomberg Business reported additional information on the alleged cyberattack on United Airlines. According to them, United Airlines detected a breach in its systems as early as May. The airline refused to comment on the report which also reported that flight manifests may have been stolen from the airline.

There is not enough data to prove that the LOT and United Airlines events are related or not. Outward appearance seems to show that the problem one airline suffered is similar to the other. Furthermore, there were gaps between the attacks and the systems were located in different parts of the world. But according to speculations, they may be linked. LOT already admitted that their issue was caused by an outside hack and not by a system failure. United Airlines, though, still hasn't admitted that the incidents were caused by cyberattacks.

While it's still unclear what the real cause of these attacks is, it can be concluded that information sharing on threat intelligence can significantly improve awareness in the airline industry and help in coming up with better defenses against evolving threats. In order to defend efficiently against cybersecurity threats, airlines need visibility into methods, variations, and origins of the attack. They must also determine the existing vulnerabilities in their systems. Through concerted investigation and sharing of information, they will be able to determine if the cybersecurity incidents are related or isolated and if steps can be taken to prevent these attacks.

Cyberattacks are getting more malicious, more sophisticated, and more dynamic. Additionally, these perpetrators share information regarding vulnerabilities and targets, and they solicit advice from a community of hackers. To reduce the risk, security professionals should have comprehensive intelligence against cyberthreats. Some critical information should be provided by security specialists coming from other organizations. In short, defenders should share information the same way that attackers do.

A tool that can be used by organizations to augment their own threat assessment is the X-Force Exchange developed by IBM. X-Force Exchange is a cloud-based, open platform wherein security professionals can share threat intelligence. X-Force Exchange has become a treasure trove of 700 TB of data containing analysis of at millions of phishing and spam attacks, billions of websites, and at least 15 billion cybersecurity events in addition to a threat intelligence network containing almost 300 million endpoints.

This massive collection of data comes with vulnerability tracking, exploits, threats from specific applications, URL reputation, IP reputation (i.e., command-and-control servers for botnets, spam sources, malware hosts), and malware information. Because it's hosted in the cloud, continuous updates on the latest intelligence information are done. Users of Exchange can gather reports which they can merge into their cybersecurity incident response, analytics platform, and forensics investigation using the system's application programming interface or social-based user interface.

In order to succeed against cyberthreats, security professionals should minimize the surface area of the attack, have threat visibility, and reduce the time it takes to react after an attack has been detected. All of these activities can become more efficient with improved threat intelligence, which can be expanded through information sharing across organizations and industries. By pooling threat data and vulnerability information, security professionals can greatly enhance their ability to avoid, detect, and divert threats.

In the near future, airlines will be able to avoid travel delays caused by cyberattacks if they improve on system vulnerabilities, attack methods, and threat collaboration efforts. IBM's X-Force Exchange can be a very useful tool in sharing threat intelligence across different industries and its intelligence vault will only increase as more entities contribute to the effort which in turn helps organizations to prepare for the next possible attack.

Chapter 23. Staying Up to Date

Cybersecurity threats are evolving and as a security professional, keeping up to date on the latest trends can be a real chore. There could be hundreds of sources out there that you can tap into and sorting through them and identifying which resources can complement your work environment and schedule can be tedious.

To stay updated about the cyberthreats lurking out there, organizations and professionals need to be able to pick out which sources can best help them prepare for potential attacks.

Here are a few tips on selecting which sources are best for you or your organization:

What type of news do you need?

The type of news that will benefit you the most will depend on a few factors. This includes your role in implementing cybersecurity. Are you an analyst, executive, or cybersecurity managers? What do you need the news for? Will you simply be passing on the information to others in the organization that will need it? Do you want to gain in-depth knowledge of the threat and how to handle it? Or do you just need to be aware? Other factors to consider are how, where, and when will you be able to get the news.

Does it just provide headlines or does it include in-depth analysis?

Some cybersecurity news sources only deliver quick headlines to their readers by aggregating feeds from different portals. These sources are great for those who just need a quick overview of current and emerging threats. A good source of headline bites for quicker digestion would itsecuritygury.org.

Front-liners, consultants, and other advanced security experts will more likely require content with in-depth analysis which they might need to use to mitigate or prevent similar threats affecting their environments. US-CERT is a favorite amongst security professionals who require more detail from their cybersecurity news.

How frequent are the news updated?

The frequency of how the news is updated is another factor that you may want to consider choosing the sources that you want to include in your regular read. There are those who would prefer that their news on emerging and existing threats be updated by the minute. Some might just need the news for informational reasons so they can get by with sources that provide updates less frequently. SANS Internet Storm Center is a good source of daily updates while Infosecurity Magazine publishes only once per month.

Is it accessible using mobile devices?

Most sources of cybersecurity news provide detailed and extensive coverage of the current thread landscape but some of them might not be optimized for viewing on mobile devices. This is particularly important if you want to get the information while you're out and about. Some cybersecurity news sites can detect if you're using a computer or a mobile device when browsing and will format the content accordingly for the best viewing experience. Some even have their own mobile apps like Cyware New. There are also curated Twitter accounts that are subscribed to top experts in the cybersecurity industry which you can follow to get a daily those of threat information via your mobile phone.

Are the cybersecurity threats classified properly?

There are threats that can be considered benign and there are those which can a lot of damage to your business. To easily determine which is which, they should be classified using a standardized system. Security news sources that categorize the threats and grades them accordingly makes life easier for front-line security professionals who need relay information on threats to stakeholders or execute mitigation strategies. Cybersecurity threats are usually classified into Distributed Denial of Service or DDoS, ransomware, phishing, Advanced Persistent Threats, etc. US-CERT is a good example of a source that classifies threats according to standards. Another one krebsonsecurity.com

Is the security industry endorsing it?

A news source must have credibility for it to be trusted by cybersecurity professionals. Those which are widely endorsed by security professionals have gained their trust and respect due to the credentials of the content creators, the quality of the news, and the overall experience. Some of the top names and the most highly respected sources in security threat news are threatbrief.com, darkreading.com, krebsonsecurity.com, and the SANS Internet Storm Center.

Chapter 24. The Future of Cybersecurity

Hacks will continue to get more and more sophisticated and attackers will be utilizing improved tools and methods to access private information. Also, technology is continuously evolving and providing a larger surface of attack for these hackers and allowing more vulnerabilities to be exploited.

The emerging trends in threat landscapes will give birth to new cybersecurity technologies and methods. More organizations are jumping into the Internet of Things or IoT, cognitive computing, and big data in a race to beat the growth of cyber threats in both complexity and quantity. The goal is to secure the devices and systems before hackers figure out how they can be exploited.

Here are some of the most significant innovations and themes shaping this interconnected world.

Big Data

As more devices are brought online, more data is produced, structured or not. The people of the world have adopted global mobilization which has popularized social networks, which also generate more data. Consequentially, data scientists were able to find ways of leveraging this huge amount of information in marketing and advertising campaigns. But others are also interested in this data with malicious intent. With hackers able to influence public behavior, there will be dire consequences.

Researchers gather data from the human brain to analyze. Sensors are put up to understand how certain emotions and stimulants affect the brain's reaction, all in the name of science. However, the data generated through these tests is extremely valuable to both scientists and hackers.

Big data might represent an enticing target for hackers but it can also be used to aid cybersecurity professionals in their fight against these perpetrators. A digital trail is always left after each criminal activity. This data can be used by security analysts to identify attackers or even predict an incoming attack. But analyzing such huge unstructured data can be daunting.

This is where cognitive security helps. Using machine learning an AI, threat data can be processed in a more efficient manner. IT professionals may even be able to predict criminal activity before it happens. And we're just scratching the surface on how cognitive computing can help shape cybersecurity in the near future.

Although many private institutions and government entities have data protection regulations implemented, the ever-evolving threat landscape calls for a complete culture change as far as security is concerned. Sensitive data should not be published on social media and people should adopt basic security solutions like antivirus software, firewalls, and password protection. These security controls should be implemented by enterprises and all employees should be trained accordingly.

Internet of Things

As a security professional, you might be well-versed in safeguarding servers and workstations or even mobile devices like smartphones and tablets. What about home automation gadgets like thermostats, refrigerators or even cars? Even hospitals are getting more connected so securing medical equipment from cyberattacks is now a real concern.

Attackers often control connected devices and group them into botnets when initiating a distributed denial-of-service or DDoS attack on high-profile websites. That's why it's important for enterprises or users to secure their devices properly. Manufacturers of such devices should bundle essential security controls with their products and businesses should extensively test their applications.

The Need for Cyber Resiliency

The damage costs due to cyberattacks are outpacing cybersecurity investment costs. Since 2016, research has shown an increase of 33% in cybercrime-related spending but increase in cybersecurity investments has only increased by 10%.

Technological innovations and digital adoption have allowed organizations to tap a wider audience than ever before. But this growth in interconnectivity is also giving more opportunities to cybercriminals to gain access to company systems and steal data. Businesses should be equipped with the proper combination of tools and knowledge in order to defend against these threats.

A report by FireEye and Marsh & McLennan emphasized the need to implement cyber resilience measures and prioritizing it over cyber defense.

Emails – The Most Common Cyberattack Vector

Employees serve an organization's frontline when it comes to cybersecurity. Unfortunately, they are also its most vulnerable component. Attackers may be able to gather sensitive data from employees by assuming false identities and sending emails that can release malware.

According to a cybersecurity study, 93% of the breaches come through pretexting and phishing and the most common entry point is via email. Also, more than ninety percent of these incidents were made possible via social engineering methods which are done by gaining the trust of people and manipulating them to give out sensitive data.

Defending from these attacks should start with user education. Users knowing how attacks can be identified are the organization's best defense against these attacks. However, awareness of these cyber risks may not be enough according to research. When users are made aware of their personal risks when they get involved in a cyberattack, they are more likely to initiate preventive actions.

Cyber Insurance

When it comes to resiliency, cyber insurance is another important part of any cyber risk strategy.

The cyber insurance market has grown significantly over the past years and premiums have increased three-fold compared to general insurance. An expected compounded 20.1% annual growth rate between 2014 to 2020 is also a realistic prediction of this lucrative business.

This increase in premium costs is due to companies who have a high-risk exposure and the insurer not having visibility on the organization's full risk profile. A cyber resilience strategy combined with protecting your data and systems discussed with the insurer can significantly decrease cyber insurance costs.

Cyber insurance can help an organization recover faster from risk activities such as data restoration, PR costs, and data breach fines. Some contracts even include social engineering fraud.

Cyber Defense Plus Cyber Resilience

It's likely that security incidents will happen sooner or later. This is why cybersecurity strategies should not only encompass avoiding attacks and breaches but also how the organization can respond systematically and intelligently when an attack happens.

There are 3 steps which can help your organization's cyber resilience:

1. Understand the vulnerabilities of the business

2. Understand the risk level that the business can absorb

3. Understand strategies and tools that can be used to safeguard against cyber threats

Putting more investment and time into coming up with strategic reactions to security incidents and recognizing that the employees as the front liner of your security defense can significantly strengthen the business' cybersecurity.

Conclusion

Cyberattacks are here to stay and they can only get more sophisticated as cybersecurity catches up. Knowing the ins-and-outs of the common attacks can be a very good foundation on how to put up an effective defense against them.

Throughout this book, we discussed a brief history of cybersecurity as well as the most common attacks today and how you can best defend against them. Case studies also provided insights into some of the most successful and damaging security attacks in the past and how they were dealt with by private and government entities. These cases also gave you an idea of how disruptive, costly, and damaging an attack can be, no matter how simple the method or how obvious the attack vector is.

As an individual or security professional who would like to have in-depth knowledge on how to defend yourself or the organization against security threats and attacks, this book contains sufficient information to guide you into that path.

But as mentioned many times throughout the book, attacks are evolving, vulnerabilities are here to stay, and hackers are getting more cunning. Therefore, you should ensure that you keep abreast of the latest security trends and keep the best security practices mentioned in this book.

Thanks for Reading!

What did you think of, **Cybersecurity: The Hacker Proof Guide To Cybersecurity, Internet Safety, Cybercrime, & Preventing Attacks**

I know you could have picked any number of books to read, but you picked this book and for that I am extremely grateful.

I hope that it added at value and quality to your everyday life. If so, it would be really nice if you could share this book with your friends and family by posting to Facebook and Twitter.

If you enjoyed this book and found some benefit in reading this, I'd like to hear from you and hope that you could take some time to post a review. Your feedback and support will help this author to greatly improve his writing craft for future projects and make this book even better.

I want you, the reader, to know that your review is very important and so, if you'd like to leave a review, all you have to do is click here and away you go. I wish you all the best in your future success!

Thank you and good luck!

Trustgenics

Claim Your Free Bonus

Master the Art of Memory Improvement with Brain Training to Learn Faster, Remember More, Increase Productivity and Improve Memory

If you've ever found yourself forgetting things then you have probably wished that your memory was better.

It transpires that there is no so such thing as a "bad" memory. There are merely people who don't use their memories to the fullest potential.

Improve your memory...read this book!